AMERICAN COURTS

_ℓ_

Daniel John Meador

James Monroe Professor of Law
University of Virginia

ST. PAUL, MINN.
WEST PUBLISHING CO.
1991

SHAQUETTA

TEXT IS PRINTED ON 10% POST
CONSUMER RECYCLED PAPER

TABLE OF CONTENTS

This little book is the result of my experiences over the years in dealing with two quite different groups of people. One has consisted of judges and lawyers from other countries; the other, of beginning American law students. These groups have in common an initial difficulty in understanding the extraordinarily complicated American judicial scene—the most complicated in the world.

It is difficult to explain to judges and lawyers from elsewhere the judicial arrangements stemming from the state-federal division of authority in the United States and the coexistence of fifty state judicial systems alongside the federal judicial system. Though American law students do have a general awareness of their country's governmental structure, they too are largely unacquainted with the organization and complexities of the multiple judicial systems. For many years I have attempted to convey to both groups, accurately and succinctly, an understanding of these matters. This book is a distillation of what I have found to be most important for this purpose.

As with a brief exposition of any complicated subject, this treatment runs the unavoidable risk of oversimplification. The book is not intended to take the place of a treatise; details and underlying explanations must be sought elsewhere.

The view of the American judiciary afforded by this book is analogous to a view of the American landscape from a jetliner on a transcontinental flight from Washington to San Francisco at 40,000 feet. From that vantage point one sees the key features—

the Blue Ridge Mountains, the Mississippi River, the Great Plains, the Rocky Mountains—but little detail. So it is with this view of the American courts; there should be enough here to give the foreigner and the beginning student the essential features. This book may also be useful to graduate and undergraduate students in government, as well as to other persons interested in the courts of this country.

The political and legal changes sweeping the world have increased interest almost everywhere in American law and government. The mobility afforded by the jet age increasingly brings lawyers and judges from other countries on visits to the United States. Many of them are eager to learn quickly about the American legal order. Thus there is a growing need for a concise yet comprehensive description of the American court systems, their structure, business, personnel, and interrelationships. My hope is that this short work can at least partly fill that need and, in so doing, further world-wide understanding of these important institutions.

At the same time, I hope to provide a helpful tool for beginning American law students, one that helps them to comprehend more quickly this complex judicial scene which they, first as students and then as lawyers, will need to understand.

DANIEL JOHN MEADOR

University of Virginia
January 1991

For editorial assistance in the preparation of this manuscript, I wish to thank my assistant, Louisa Dixon, and my student research assistant, Jordana Simone Bernstein, Class of 1992, University of Virginia School of Law. I am indebted also to my colleague, Professor Graham C. Lilly, for numerous helpful suggestions.

CHAPTER ONE

INTRODUCTORY OVERVIEW

American courts are not embraced within a single judicial or governmental structure. Properly speaking, there is no such thing as *the* American judicial system. Instead, there are multiple systems, each independent of the others. There are also multiple sources of American law. The courts of one system are often called upon to apply and interpret the law generated in another. Moreover, there is often duplicative, concurrent jurisdiction over the same case in two or more judicial systems. These circumstances and others combine to give the United States its extraordinarily complicated legal order.

The great divide in the American legal landscape is the state-federal line. It derives from the United States Constitution, pursuant to which the federal government was created in 1789 to "form a more perfect Union" of the existing states. The federal government and the state governments coexist, with a broad range of powers delegated to the former and all others reserved to the latter. Each of these governments has its own court system, autonomous and self-contained.

Today there are fifty states and thus fifty state judicial systems. Separate court systems, analogous to those in the states, are maintained in the District of Columbia and the Commonwealth of Puerto Rico. There are also territorial courts in the Virgin Islands, Guam, American Samoa, and the Northern Mariana

1

Islands. Collectively, these American courts extend over an immense geographical expanse, from the northeastern seaboard in Maine to the far Pacific islands and from Puerto Rico to Alaska.

The federal judiciary and the fifty state judicial systems are each constructed like a pyramid. In broad outline these systems are similar, but they vary in the details of their organization and business. Across the base are the trial courts, the courts of first instance. At the apex is the court of last resort, usually called the supreme court. In most states and in the federal system there is a middle tier, the intermediate appellate courts. All of these courts draw their style and their conceptions of judicial power from the English common-law and equity courts, the legal order that was transplanted to North American shores by the British colonists in the seventeenth and eighteenth centuries. Louisiana, however, is a unique hybrid because of its roots in the French civil-law system.

Two features distinguish American courts from the English courts and from those of any other country: the separation of powers and the doctrine of judicial review. The American concept of the separation of powers calls for all governmental authority to be divided into three parts—legislative, executive, and judicial. Each part must be in the hands of different officials or official bodies. Put in its simplest form, the doctrine requires that the legislative branch make the law through the passage of statutes, the executive branch enforce the law, and the judicial branch interpret and enunciate the meaning of the law through the adjudication of disputes. By thus dividing power, the doctrine aims to protect citizens from abuses of official authority stemming from its concentration in the hands of too few persons or in a single body. In the mystique of American politics, this arrangement is viewed as fundamental to liberty and to government under law. It is embodied in all American governmental structures; hence, the set of federal and state courts functions as a separate branch of government, independent of the legislative and executive branches.

The other distinctive feature of American courts is the doctrine of judicial review. Under this doctrine, a court has power to hold a legislative act (a statute) to be contrary to either the Federal Constitution or a state constitution and hence unenforceable. Similarly, courts also exercise power to hold unconstitutional the acts of executive officials. Constitutional adjudications of these sorts can occur in any civil or criminal case. There are no special constitutional courts in the United States. Any court, state or federal, can pass on the constitutionality of a statute or of executive action, state or federal, whenever the question is necessary to the resolution of a case before it. State courts must apply both the state constitution and the Federal Constitution; if there is any conflict between the two, the Federal Constitution will prevail. Federal courts apply the Federal Constitution; they also have authority to apply state constitutional provisions when the meaning of such provisions is drawn in question, but they will normally defer to state courts on a question of that sort. The power of judicial review, unknown in England and not employed by the ordinary courts in civil-law countries, clothes American courts with the authority to set aside actions of the elected representatives of the people on the ground that they are contrary to the higher law of the constitution.

Judicial review and separation of powers are major elements in the American conception of the "rule of law." They guarantee an independent judiciary authorized to apply the basic charters of government to control executive and legislative action. The rule of law also implies a body of principles, standards, and rules to which all are subject and which will be applied objectively by independent judges acting through established procedures. The legal order, as ultimately enforced by the courts, embraces all; no one is above, below, or outside the law.

The United States, with its English legal inheritance, is known as a "common-law country." This means that case law has traditionally formed a large part of the legal corpus administered in American courts. This case law is the body of legal principles and rules derived from the written opinions issued by intermediate appellate courts and courts of last resort to explain their decisions. Under the doctrine of precedent, or stare decisis, these decisions are binding in later cases unless they can be distinguished or, as occasionally happens, overruled. Although case law remains a major part of American jurisprudence, litigation is now as likely to involve enactments of federal and state legislative bodies (statutory law) as it is to involve common-law rules (case law). In addition to statutory enactments, regulations issued by various administrative agencies have proliferated, and they too are frequently involved in litigated controversies.

When opinions of American courts are published, they are collected in various sets of bound volumes known as reports. Most states have their own official reports, and decisions from all states are included in regional reports provided by private publishers for the convenience of users. There are other reports for federal decisions. Legislative enactments are published separately. In each state there is a multi-volume set of its statutes, sometimes referred to as its code. Federal statutes are compiled in the *United States Code*. There are also multitudes of published volumes of administrative regulations in both the federal and state spheres.

In addition to being published in bound volumes, many court decisions, statutes, and regulations are now available nationwide through electronic data retrieval systems. The two major systems of this sort are WESTLAW and LEXIS. The statutes and regulations, combined with the reports of court decisions, constitute a formidable mass of material that American lawyers and judges must research and analyze. Furthermore, each judicial system has its own written rules of civil and criminal procedure that must be followed in all the courts of that system.

American courts adhere to the adversary process, as distinguished from the inquisitorial process that prevails on the continent of Europe and in numerous countries elsewhere. In both civil and criminal cases, the parties through their lawyers are solely responsible for presenting the facts to the court. In civil cases, before trial both parties' attorneys may conduct discovery—identifying witnesses, gathering relevant information, and learning about the opposing party's witnesses and evidence. A large majority of civil actions are disposed of at this pretrial stage; only some 5 to 10% actually go to trial. At trial the lawyers call and question the witnesses. The testimony elicited in court, along with all other items admitted into evidence by the judge, forms the trial record. Based on this adversarial "party presentation," the trial court makes determinations of fact, applies the pertinent law, and enters judgment accordingly.

If either party is dissatisfied with the outcome of the case, he may appeal. Although a large proportion of all criminal convictions are appealed, only a relatively small percentage of judgments in civil cases are taken beyond the trial court. Appeals are based solely on the record made in the trial court. No witnesses appear and no new evidence can be offered at the appellate level; normally no questions can be raised there for the first time. Unlike trial courts, over which a single judge presides, appellate courts are multi-judge forums acting collegially. Appellate courts generally confine themselves to reviewing questions of law raised in the trial court proceedings; factual determinations made by the trial court are not normally disturbed. The appellate court's sole function is to determine whether, as a matter of law, the trial court's judgment should be affirmed, reversed, or modified in some way. If the appellate court concludes that the lower court erred in its application of the law, the appellate court may reverse the lower court's decision. It will do so unless the reviewing judges conclude that the error was relatively minor and probably did not affect the outcome in the trial court.

The dominant concern in American courts since the 1960s has been the ever-increasing rise in the quantity of cases. While this growth has varied from one place to another, it has been significant almost everywhere. In many trial courts the number of cases commenced annually has tripled over the past three decades. As a result, delays in getting to trial can be lengthy, running up to five years in some courts. In many appellate courts the increase in caseload has been even greater. Although the explanation for this growth is not clear, this crisis of volume appears to result from a combination of an expanding population, rising affluence and mobility among the American people, spreading governmental regulation, erosion in the influence of family, neighborhood, church, school, and other institutions, and a heightened contentiousness among racial, religious, and other groups in society. Whatever the cause, the rising tide of litigation has engendered additional numbers and types of personnel in the courts and modifications in judicial procedures.

The major change in trial courts has been the introduction of affirmative case management by judges. The tradition in the common-law adversarial system of letting the opposing lawyers control the progress of cases, with the judge being merely a passive umpire, has been significantly altered in many of the busiest trial courts. Today many judges hold conferences with parties' lawyers to take control of cases at an early stage, setting schedules for pretrial activities and often encouraging settlement discussions, all for the purpose of moving cases to conclusion without undue delay and expense. While this development has been somewhat controversial, many judges and court administrators believe that such judicial management is essential to avoid unreasonable backlogs of cases.

At the appellate level two new developments have resulted from the unprecedented rise in the quantity of appeals. One is the employment of central staff attorneys—lawyers working for the court as an entity (as distinguished from law clerks who are legal assistants working directly with individual judges)—to screen appeals preliminarily, to prepare memoranda on the cases, and sometimes to draft proposed opinions. The other development has been the introduction of truncated processes. These typically involve the routing of appeals deemed to be relatively simple through a shortened process that may involve no oral argument and no formal conference of the judges, leaving the court to rely primarily on the lawyers' written submissions (briefs) or staff-prepared memoranda. The opinion in this type of case is likely to be terse, without elaborate discussion about the judges' reasoning. The more difficult and complicated cases, on the other hand, are routed through the traditional appellate process (oral argument, conference of the judges, fully explanatory opinion). In many appellate courts today, over half of the appeals are decided without oral argument, and a sizable number are decided by a short written statement giving little or no explanation for the decision. Most such decisions are not included in the published reports.

Despite the increase in litigation and the changes it has wrought, the right to jury trial remains a key feature of American procedure. The jury is the means whereby citizens are involved in the judicial process. Traditionally juries consisted of twelve persons. An evolution has occurred in that respect, however, and today juries are often of fewer numbers, but usually no smaller than six. Laypersons never sit with judges as members of the court, and juries do not participate at the appellate level. The jury's role is to decide contested issues of fact; the judge decides the issues of law. The jury functions under the control of the judge. The judge instructs the jury as to what it is to do, and he has the authority to set aside the jury's verdict if he thinks the jury acted improperly.

In all of the federal and state courts, a defendant charged with a serious crime has a right to trial by jury. In civil litigation, either party has a right to trial by jury in cases of the type inherited from the English common-law courts, typically cases in which money damages or the recovery of property is the remedy being sought. In other civil cases, largely those of the type heard in the English Court of Chancery, there is no right to trial by jury; typically the remedy sought in these equity cases is an injunction, an order by the court requiring the defendant to do or not to do something. Some cases are mixed; that is, the plaintiff seeks both money damages and an injunction. In most such cases there is a right to trial by jury.

The state courts are the front-line adjudicators in the United States. They overshadow the federal courts in both the number of cases they handle and the number of persons involved as litigants, lawyers, and judges. In the trial courts of the fifty states more than 29,000,000 cases, civil and criminal, are filed annually, compared with fewer than 300,000 in the federal trial courts. In other words, there are nearly one hundred times as many cases commenced in the state courts as in the federal courts. In numbers of judges, the state courts likewise eclipse the federal. There are over 27,000 judges in the state trial courts, while there are little more than 1,000 federal trial judges.

Although in volume of business and number of judicial personnel the federal courts are far smaller than the state courts collectively, those figures belie the importance of the federal courts; much of their business significantly affects the operations of government throughout the country and touches the lives of many persons well beyond the parties in particular cases. Still, for the average citizen in the great mass of everyday affairs the main courts are the state courts.

It is appropriate, therefore, to proceed in Chapter Two with a description of the state court systems, their structure, and the nature of their work. Chapter Three then similarly describes the federal court system. Next, Chapter Four sketches some of the complications stemming from these multiple judiciaries' functioning together in contemporary American society. Chapter Five describes the judges and other persons, including lawyers for litigants, involved in the work of American courts. Finally, Chapter Six indicates some of the trends and possible future directions concerning American courts. The appendices provide additional details on court structures and types of courts and judgeships in the fifty states and the federal judiciary. For those interested in pursuing the subject further, a list of selected readings and sources appears in Appendix E.

CHAPTER TWO

THE STATE COURTS

Each of the fifty states has its own written constitution. These documents, like the Federal Constitution, embody the principle of separation of powers, establishing the state's legislature (sometimes called the General Assembly) as the lawmaking body, the Governor as the chief executive officer, and a court system to exercise the judicial power. In some states the constitution itself creates the entire court system at both trial and appellate levels. In others the constitution does little more than authorize the legislature to establish the judicial structure.

Whether created by the state constitution or by enactments of the legislature, the judicial systems of the fifty states resemble each other in broad outline. Like all other aspects of state governments, however, they vary in detail. Any generalizations risk the portrayal of a judicial structure that is not quite like that in some or even many states. What follows is a description of the key components of the state court systems, with an indication of the typical patterns and variations. Diagrams of five state judicial systems, illustrating the variations, are contained in Appendix A. Tables listing the courts in each of the fifty states, with the number of judges on each court, are contained in Appendix B.

Trial Courts

The trial courts are the lowest courts in all state systems, forming the base of the judicial pyramid. They are the most numerous courts, and collectively they have the most judges and cases. They are spread throughout the cities and counties in the state. These are the courts in which lawsuits are initially filed; hence, they are referred to as courts of "first instance" or courts of "original jurisdiction." When persons commence civil proceedings, and when the state commences criminal prosecutions, they do so in trial courts.

In most states this base of courts of first instance is subdivided into two levels. The major trial courts, the upper level, are referred to as courts of "general jurisdiction" because they have authority to hear and decide numerous types of cases, civil and criminal. Unless some statutory or constitutional provision specifically deprives them of jurisdiction, they typically can adjudicate any kind of case. The name given these courts varies from one state to another. In some states they are called "circuit courts"; in other states they are known as "superior courts"; in still others they are "district courts." This lack of uniformity in terminology is one of the many factors contributing to confusion concerning American courts.

The lower level of trial courts, below the courts of general jurisdiction, consists of courts of "limited jurisdiction." In contrast to courts of general jurisdiction, these courts have relatively restricted authority. Typically such a court has power to adjudicate only a narrow range of matters, often only one specific type of case. For example, in some states there are traffic courts vested with jurisdiction over relatively minor motor vehicle offenses. In some states there are probate courts with authority only over the administration of decedents' estates or over guardianships of minors and incompetents. The authority of some courts of limited jurisdiction is defined in monetary terms. For example, a "small claims court" may have jurisdiction over civil cases in which the damages do not exceed $5,000 or some other relatively small amount. States typically maintain courts of limited jurisdiction to try misdemeanors and perhaps juvenile offenses that are not serious. Here again there is considerable variation from one state to another.

The term *limited jurisdiction* does not necessarily mean that the court's business is confined to small-scale matters or that all of its business is necessarily less important than that of general jurisdiction courts. A probate court can administer estates worth millions of dollars. Family courts found in some states have authority to grant divorces, determine custody of children, fix alimony and child support, and decide a variety of other matters concerning the family. Some states have a hodgepodge of limited jurisdiction courts (usually resulting from the legislature's unsystematic creation of special courts from time to time) such as trial courts for designated municipalities as well as numerous courts of the types just mentioned (e.g., Georgia, p. 87). In such states the line between general and limited jurisdiction courts tends to become blurred. In other states the legislature has grouped all limited jurisdiction courts into a single lower trial level, thus eliminating the multiple courts with different jurisdictions (e.g., Virginia, p. 90). Whatever their structure, limited jurisdiction courts handle a far greater volume of cases than general jurisdiction courts—approximately six times as many in most states.

A major twentieth-century movement has been aimed at unifying state trial courts. Its key feature is the consolidation of all trial court business into a single judicial tier, thereby abolishing the distinction between the two trial levels (e.g., Illinois and Iowa, pp. 88 and 89). Some states that have unified their trial courts in form have at the same time organized the supposedly single, unified court into divisions such as the probate division, family division, small claims division, and so on, thereby preserving in substance the structure of the old limited jurisdiction courts. However, having all trial courts grouped into one tier, even nominally, permits a more effective management of trial level business. Under a single administrative authority, judges can be assigned from one division to another as the work requires. It is thought that a unified trial court also serves to avoid the appearance of second-class justice for cases that would otherwise be handled by courts of limited jurisdiction.

Whether organized into one level or two, these courts of first instance are the forums in which cases are initially heard and decided. As explained in the previous chapter, it is here that witnesses are called to testify, and it is here that controverted facts are resolved. In state trial courts factual issues are resolved either by a jury or by the trial judge alone if there is no right to a jury or if the parties waive the right. The judgment, entered in accordance with the applicable law and the facts that have been established, authoritatively settles the dispute between the parties. However, the judgments of trial courts are subject to review and possible reversal by courts above them in the judicial hierarchy. For some courts of limited jurisdiction the first review is in the upper level trial court. For the trial courts of general jurisdiction, and sometimes for lower trial courts, review is in the appellate courts. Because many cases are not appealed, especially those resolved in the limited jurisdiction courts, the trial courts are the final adjudicators of the large majority of all controversies entering the state judicial systems.

Appellate Courts

At the apex of the judicial pyramid in every state is the court of last resort, usually called the supreme court. There are only a few exceptions to this terminology. In New York and Maryland the highest tribunal is named the Court of Appeals, and in Massachusetts and Maine it is known as the Supreme Judicial Court. In two states, Texas and Oklahoma, there are two courts of last resort: the Supreme Court (for civil cases) and the Court of Criminal Appeals (for criminal cases). Most state courts of last resort have seven judges, usually called "justices." The smallest has three and the largest, nine. In a few states these courts function in panels of fewer than all their members. However, in most states all judges usually sit together so that the court functions as a unit when hearing and deciding appeals.

Originally a state's supreme court was the only appellate court in the state. It had jurisdiction over all appeals from the state's trial courts. In the late nineteenth century the rising tide of litigation began to overrun the capacity of the single supreme court in some states. In response the legislatures began to create intermediate appellate courts. These courts were inserted as a new judicial tier between the trial courts of general jurisdiction and the supreme court. Although the name given these courts varies, the most common title is court of appeals. Until well into the twentieth century only a minority of states had established such courts. The movement to create them quickened after the Second World War; today thirty-eight states have intermediate appellate courts.

The major purpose in establishing this new judicial tier was to increase the appellate capacity of the judicial system. In most states the intermediate courts are designed to handle the great mass of appeals, to act as the "work horses" of the appellate system. The state supreme court is thereby reserved for decision of the more important cases, usually those of significance to the law and the administration of justice and not solely of interest to the litigants.

States have constructed the intermediate appellate level in various ways. Some states have a single intermediate court of statewide jurisdiction, deciding both civil and criminal appeals from trial courts throughout the state (e.g., Georgia, p. 87; Virginia, p. 90). In other states there are multiple intermediate courts, organized into geographical districts, each with jurisdiction over appeals from the trial courts within its district (e.g., California, p. 86; Illinois, p. 88). In a few states the intermediate tier is divided by subject matter rather than along territorial lines. Alabama, for example, has one court of appeals for civil cases and another for criminal cases. Pennsylvania has one appellate court for cases involving administrative agencies and local government entities and another for appeals in all other cases.

Regardless of whether the intermediate courts are organized on a statewide, geographical, or subject-matter basis, they all generally sit in three-judge panels for the purpose of hearing and deciding appeals. Many of these courts now have considerably more than three judges. It is common to find intermediate appellate courts with ten to fifteen judges; often there are many more. In New Jersey and Michigan the single statewide courts have twenty-eight and eighteen judges respectively. In states in which the appellate courts sit in geographical districts, each district may have a dozen or more judges, functioning through three-judge panels, with the statewide total of appellate judges being many times larger. California, for example, has a total of eighty-eight judges in its six autonomous appellate districts. In each appellate court, whether district or statewide, a decision of a three-judge panel is generally in the name of the full court. States vary, however, as to whether a panel is bound to follow a prior decision of another panel of that same court. When conflicting rulings on the same question of law develop among panels, the only means of resolving such conflicts is usually by way of review in the state supreme court.

When a state legislature establishes an intermediate appellate level in its judicial system, it must make several decisions concerning the relationship of the intermediate court to the supreme court. These are decisions as to how the state's appellate work is to be routed from the trial courts and how it is to be distributed between the two appellate levels. Various arrangements can be found among the states.

The simplest scheme is to provide that all appeals from the trial courts go to the intermediate court, with the supreme court receiving no appeals directly from the trial level. The supreme court's jurisdiction is limited to reviewing the intermediate court's decisions on a discretionary basis. That is, after the appeal has been decided in the intermediate court, the losing litigant may petition the supreme court for review. That court may then, in its discretion, decide whether to take up the case for decision.

The theory of this arrangement is that every litigant is entitled to one appellate review of a trial court's judgment on the merits, and that review is to be provided by the intermediate court. But, so the theory goes, a litigant is not entitled as a matter of right to two appeals; any further review after the first appeal should be provided only in the interest of the law and the legal system. Thus the supreme court is given discretion to determine what cases, among the large number in which petitions are filed, deserve its attention in its institutional law-developing role, leaving the bulk of appeals to the error-correcting function of the intermediate court.

This is the jurisdictional arrangement favored in the American Bar Association's Standards of Judicial Administration, an influential set of recommended structures, and it is favored by numerous court reformers. However, few states have a pure scheme of that sort. In numerous states there are provisions for certain types of cases to be appealed as a matter of right from the trial court to the supreme court, bypassing the intermediate court. Criminal cases in which the death sentence has been imposed are often treated this way. In some states this "by-pass" jurisdiction is provided for cases in which the trial court has held a state or federal statute unconstitutional. The theory is that cases of these types are so important, and so likely to reach the supreme court in any event, that economy of judicial effort is served ánd justice expedited by routing them there in the first instance.

Intermediate courts are often given authority to certify cases to the supreme court for decision. The reason is that the intermediate court, after an appeal is filed there, may perceive that the matter is of such urgency and importance that it should be resolved by the state's highest court without the delay that would be involved in the intermediate court's first hearing and deciding the matter. In some states such "certification" jurisdiction extends to the whole case; in other states it extends only to specific questions, and the intermediate court retains the case pending the supreme court's answer.

In some states the supreme court has authority to transfer to itself, on its own motion, a case pending in the intermediate court. Sometimes referred to as "reach-down" jurisdiction, this power makes it possible for the top court to take jurisdiction over a case without waiting for certification by the intermediate court or a petition from a party. This discretionary authority can be exercised either because of the urgency and importance of the matter or to relieve a congestion of cases in the intermediate court.

In most states there is some combination of these jurisdictional provisions. Typically, most appeals go initially as a matter of right to the intermediate court and are subject to discretionary review thereafter in the supreme court. But there is also typically some by-pass jurisdiction for at least a few categories of cases, and there is often certification and reach-down authority. The arrangements for allocating appellate jurisdiction between the two appellate levels vary so much in detail from one state to another that it is difficult to generalize with accuracy.

Still another way of managing appellate business in a state with an intermediate court is to have initial supreme court control over all appeals. Under that arrangement, found in several states, all appeals are filed initially in the supreme court. That court screens the cases, retaining some and referring others to the intermediate court for decision. In other words, appeals come to the intermediate court only by "reference" from the supreme court (e.g., Iowa, p. 89). The rationale is that the supreme court can best determine which cases are institutionally significant, hence warranting its attention, and which cases are more routine and thus appropriate for the error-correcting function of the intermediate court.

The error-correcting and lawmaking roles often ascribed respectively to intermediate courts and courts of last resort are not clearly separable. Under that theoretical dichotomy the top court is responsible for maintaining statewide uniformity in the law and for the ongoing development of the law; it is not primarily concerned with correcting errors in the interest of individual litigants. The assumption is that the common-law type of judicial lawmaking takes place mainly in the court of last resort. But in passing on alleged errors the intermediate court inevitably "makes law" in the common-law fashion, even though many of its decisions concern relatively routine questions and have little precedential value. Just as intermediate courts are aware of their lawmaking function, so too are supreme courts aware of the need to ensure that a case has been correctly resolved. Thus it is not rare to find a supreme court taking up a case because its judges believe that a serious error has been committed below, even though the case has no larger significance for the law.

The Business of the State Courts

When state courts came into being in the thirteen former British colonies, each of these judicial systems was autonomous, and there was no coexisting national judiciary spanning the states. After the ratification of the United States Constitution and the formation of the federal government in 1789, the state court systems continued as before with all the jurisdiction that they already possessed; the federal courts did not supplant the state courts. As Alexander Hamilton wrote in *The Federalist* No. 82, under the federal constitutional scheme the state courts would retain all of their preexisting authority except to the extent that the Constitution or laws of the United States took such authority away from them. The Constitution itself did not expressly deprive state courts of any jurisdiction, and early federal statutes made only minimal exclusions of state jurisdiction. Thus the creation of the Federal Union left state court authority essentially unimpaired. As new states were formed and admitted to the Union, they came with judicial systems of their own, possessing the full range of jurisdiction that the older states exercised.

The business of the state courts was and is to a large extent the business of the English common-law courts and the English Court of Chancery. English law and equity, substantively and procedurally, were transplanted to North America where they took root, although not every feature of that jurisprudence survived. Over time, through the evolutionary process of case-by-case adjudication and occasionally by the enactment of statutes, law and equity took on a distinctively American cast. But in major outline and key features, this inherited body of jurisprudence still underlies a large part of the work of the fifty state court systems.

The entire domain of private rights with which English law and equity were concerned is the province of state courts. New areas of private law (the law concerned with disputes between citizens, as distinguished from disputes between citizens and government) have been developed over the decades through statutes and judicial decisions; these too come within state court authority. For the typical citizen or business entity caught up in a legal controversy, the state courts are likely to be the forums to which recourse will be had.

On the civil side, suits in tort, such as actions for assault and battery, negligence, and defamation, form a large part of state court business, as do controversies over rights to property, suits for breach of contract, and actions for divorce, alimony, and child custody. Disputes arising out of trusts, decedents' estates, commercial transactions, and the activities of private corporations also constitute a significant part of state court work. In short, the great bulk of everyday individual and business activities provides grist for the state courts. In addition, controversies arising out of state administrative regulations come before the state courts. The relief the courts give in civil cases can be a judgment for money to compensate a party for the injury suffered, a judgment restoring or confirming title to property, a "declaratory judgment" that defines the rights and liabilities of the parties, or an order, such as an injunction, directing a party to do or to cease doing something.

Criminal cases constitute the other substantial part of state court business. In the American governmental scheme the maintenance of basic order is a state, not a federal, responsibility. Thus the major and most common crimes come within state court jurisdiction. These include homicide, rape, robbery, larceny, embezzlement, and assault and battery. These and other felonious breaches of state law are prosecuted in the trial courts of general jurisdiction. Misdemeanors and a host of minor offenses such as traffic violations are typically prosecuted in courts of limited jurisdiction.

While state courts are concerned primarily with adjudicating cases governed by state law, they are increasingly involved in deciding questions of federal law. The supremacy clause in article VI of the Federal Constitution provides that the Constitution and the laws and treaties made pursuant thereto, "shall be the supreme Law of the Land; and the Judges in every State shall be bound thereby." Thus, whenever a provision of the Federal Constitution, a treaty, or an act of Congress is relied upon by a party in a state case, the state court is required to interpret it and give it effect if it is applicable.

Federal law can be involved in state litigation in several ways. In civil cases the plaintiff's suit might be based on federal statutory or constitutional law. Congress has enacted many statutes creating private rights of action; state courts have jurisdiction over such actions unless Congress has expressly prohibited state jurisdiction, and in many statutes such jurisdiction is not prohibited. In certain circumstances, plaintiffs can assert claims in state courts grounded directly on the Federal Constitution. Such claims are often made against state officials and agencies for alleged violations of the fourteenth amendment, which prohibits the states from depriving any person of life, liberty, or property without due process of law and from denying to any person the equal protection of the laws. Federal law can also be injected into a case by the defendant; in a civil action brought under state law the defendant may assert a defense based on federal law.

The majority of federal questions decided by state courts arise in criminal prosecutions. This results from the expansive interpretation the United States Supreme Court has given the fourteenth amendment to the Federal Constitution. The Court has construed the due process and equal protection clauses of that amendment to accord state criminal defendants a wide range of rights. It is almost routine for a defendant in a state criminal case to assert some defense or right rooted in the Federal Constitution.

These legislative and judicial developments at the federal level have caused a marked increase in the number of federal questions involved in state cases. A study by the National Center for State Courts showed that in the twenty-year period from 1959 to 1979 the number of federal questions in state supreme court opinions tripled. An independent survey in 1983 indicated that federal questions were decided in more than 25% of published state supreme court opinions.

Most of the civil cases litigated in state courts arise under the law of the state in which the court sits. But state courts of general jurisdiction are not confined to such cases. In addition to adjudicating civil actions arising under federal law, state courts can entertain cases arising under the laws of other states and of foreign countries. Assuming that it has jurisdiction over the defendant, a state trial court sitting in Virginia, for example, can hear and decide cases arising under New York law or California law or under the law of England or Germany or Japan. These and other complicating circumstances will be discussed in Chapter Four.

First, however, it is necessary to describe the coexisting federal judicial system.

CHAPTER THREE

THE FEDERAL COURTS

Article III of the Federal Constitution provides: "The judicial Power of the United States, shall be vested in one supreme Court, and in such inferior Courts as the Congress may from time to time ordain and establish." (Article III is set out in its entirety in Appendix D.) Thus by its terms the Constitution purports to establish the Supreme Court but no other courts. The creation of other federal courts is left up to Congress. That body moved promptly to pass the Judiciary Act of 1789, setting up the federal judicial system with trial courts in every state. The first set of intermediate courts with purely appellate jurisdiction was established by Congress in 1891. The structure put in place then is essentially the structure that exists today.

The federal judicial pyramid, like that in many states, is three-tiered. At the base are the trial courts, the major ones being the district courts. At the middle level are the courts of appeals. At the apex is the Supreme Court. These will be described in turn.

District Courts

In its design for the federal judiciary, Congress has divided the United States and its territories into ninety-four federal judicial districts. There is at least one such district in each state. In the largest and most heavily populated states there are several districts, identified geographically by such designations as the Southern

23

District of New York. With minor exceptions, no judicial district crosses state lines.

In each district there is a United States District Court. These ninety-four courts are the major trial courts of the federal judiciary. Each of these courts has at least two judges; many have several, and in the most populous districts the court has more than two dozen. (A list of the judicial districts and the number of judges in each is contained in Appendix C.) Because each district covers either an entire state or a large part of a state, the court typically holds sessions in several cities in the district. For example, the United States District Court for the Eastern District of Virginia (covering the eastern half of the state) sits in Richmond, Norfolk, and Alexandria.

Although a district court may have numerous judges, each case is presided over by a single judge, as in the state trial courts. In civil actions seeking money damages, the Constitution guarantees a right to jury trial if a jury is requested by either party. Statutes sometimes accord a right to jury trial in other cases. If the right to jury trial is waived, or if no such right is given by the Constitution or a statute, the judge acts as trier of fact as well as of law. Criminal prosecutions, other than for misdemeanors, are conducted with juries unless the defendant waives that right.

Within the district courts there are subordinate judicial officers known as federal magistrate judges. Proceedings conducted by these judicial officers provide for the federal judiciary something akin to courts of limited jurisdiction in the state systems. However, the judgments entered by magistrate judges are considered judgments of the district court, not those of an inferior court. Magistrate judges are described further in Chapter Five.

Courts of Appeals

In addition to having created the ninety-four districts as units of trial court organization, Congress has also established thirteen federal judicial circuits as a basis for the federal intermediate court structure. In each circuit there is a court of appeals, officially designated as the United States Court of Appeals for that circuit. Eleven of the circuits are numbered and are organized on a territorial basis, each embracing several states. For example, the Fourth Circuit includes the states of Maryland, Virginia, West Virginia, North Carolina, and South Carolina. (See map, p. 26.) The United States Court of Appeals for the District of Columbia Circuit embraces only the District of Columbia. The court of appeals in each geographical circuit has jurisdiction over appeals from the district courts within its circuit, in both civil and criminal cases. These courts also have jurisdiction to review orders of the major federal administrative agencies, although in practice most of this agency review is concentrated in the D.C. Circuit.

The only federal appellate court not organized on a territorial basis is the United States Court of Appeals for the Federal Circuit. That court's jurisdiction is defined in part by the subject matter of cases. It has jurisdiction over appeals from all ninety-four district courts in cases arising under the patent laws and in certain damage suits against the federal government. In addition it has jurisdiction over appeals from several administrative agencies and from decisions of two special trial courts: the Claims Court and the Court of International Trade.

The number of judges on each of these thirteen appellate courts varies considerably, from six in the First Circuit to twenty-eight in the Ninth. Most circuits have between ten and fifteen. Regardless of the total number of judges, each court of appeals always hears and decides cases in panels of three. The composition of these panels is constantly changed so that the judges sit from month to month in different threesomes. In the event of conflicting decisions between two or more panels on the same legal question, or when there is a question of unusual importance, the court has authority to hear or rehear the case en banc. That is, the case can be heard and decided by all active judges of the court. A federal statute provides that any court of appeals with more

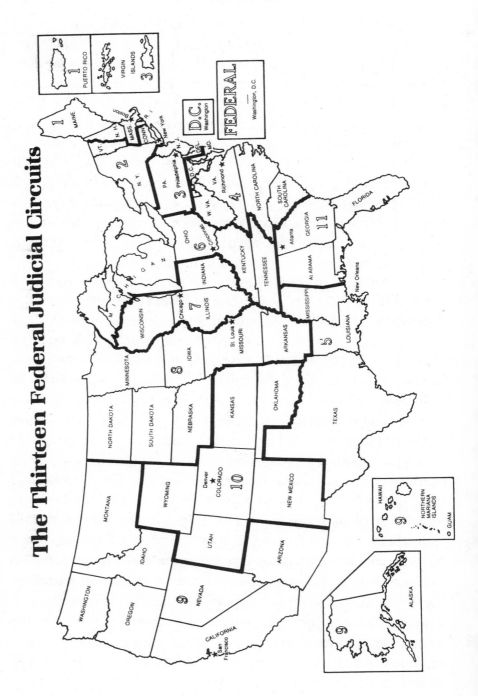

The Thirteen Federal Judicial Circuits

than fifteen judges can sit en banc with fewer than all its judges, in such number as the court may fix. The Court of Appeals for the Ninth Circuit is the only court to take such a step, holding en banc hearings with eleven of its twenty-eight judges.

Appendix C shows each court of appeals, the number of its judges, and the judicial districts over which it has jurisdiction.

Supreme Court

At the apex of the federal judicial pyramid is the Supreme Court of the United States, the only court specifically provided for in the Constitution. Legislation enacted by Congress sets the number of its judges (called Justices) and its jurisdiction, within the boundaries of the jurisdiction authorized by article III of the Constitution.

The Court has—and has had since the middle of the nineteenth century—nine Justices, one of whom is designated as the Chief Justice of the United States. The Court sits in Washington in a building of its own, just east of the Capitol. It opens its annual term on the first Monday in October and normally adjourns at the end of June.

The Supreme Court has jurisdiction to review all decisions of the federal appellate courts. It also has jurisdiction over decisions of the highest state courts when those courts have decided a question of federal law. The power to review cases from both state and federal courts gives the Supreme Court a unique position in the American judiciary's firmament.

With minor exceptions, the Court's jurisdiction is discretionary. Litigants petition the Court for a writ of certiorari, in effect asking the Court to hear and decide a case on its merits. The Court then, in its discretion, decides whether to do so. In this process the Court employs a "rule of four." If any four of the nine Justices wish to grant the writ of certiorari, the case will be taken up for decision. Otherwise, certiorari is denied, and the decision of the court below is left standing.

A denial of certiorari does not imply that the Supreme Court believes that the lower court correctly decided the merits of the case; it simply means that the legal issue raised by the case is not one that the Court wishes to address—at least at the time it denies review. Perhaps its docket is too crowded to add an additional case, the question raised by the case is not a significant one, the facts of the case do not pose the issue clearly, or the Court wishes to await further consideration of the issue by other courts so that it will have the benefit of other judges' reasoning.

If certiorari is granted, the case is scheduled for hearing. Briefs will be filed by the opposing parties, oral argument will be presented by counsel to the full Court, and the case will be decided by a written opinion. In all of its work—acting on certiorari petitions, hearing arguments, and deciding cases—the Supreme Court always acts through all nine Justices; it never functions in panels.

Normally the Supreme Court reviews a case from a federal court of appeals only after that court has rendered its decision. Although the Court can grant certiorari to review a case before the court of appeals has reached a decision, this authority is exercised sparingly and only when there is special urgency involving a matter of great public importance. There is only one circumstance in which the Supreme Court can review a district court case directly. When a district court sits with three judges, as it is authorized to do in certain instances, an appeal can be taken directly to the Supreme Court.

The Supreme Court's jurisdiction over state courts is confined to reviewing decisions of the highest court of a state involving a controlling question of federal law. A federal question is controlling if the Supreme Court's reversal of the state court's determination of that question would necessarily reverse the entire judgment. The federal law could be either statutory or constitutional. This, in effect, gives the Supreme Court authority to oversee the decisions of the fifty state supreme courts insofar as federal law is concerned. This jurisdiction extends also to the courts of the District of Columbia and the Commonwealth of Puerto Rico. The Supreme Court has no jurisdiction to decide state law questions in cases coming from the state courts; in each state, the state supreme court is the final and authoritative expositor of that state's law.

To sum up, the United States Supreme Court has jurisdiction over sixty-five appellate courts: the thirteen United States courts of appeals (as to all types of questions) and the fifty state supreme courts, the Court of Appeals of the District of Columbia, and the Supreme Court of Puerto Rico (as to federal questions). Probably no other appellate court in the world has such extensive jurisdiction over other appellate courts.

Other Federal Courts

All of the courts described above, forming the basic federal judicial pyramid, are courts established pursuant to article III of the Constitution. That is, they are courts whose judges hold office "during good behavior," not for specified terms of years, and whose compensation cannot be reduced. These courts can exercise no authority beyond that which is specified in article III. These are the courts usually referred to collectively as the federal judiciary or the federal judicial system.

Congress has occasionally established other article III courts. One is the Court of International Trade, a trial court that exercises jurisdiction over a variety of cases arising under the laws concerning customs duties and importation of goods. It has permanent judges of its own. There are two special article III courts without their own judges; cases in those courts are heard by judges from other article III courts sitting temporarily by designation of the Chief Justice of the United States. One is the Temporary Emergency Court of Appeals, which hears appeals from district courts throughout the country in certain cases arising under the federal energy regulations. Another such special court is the

Foreign Intelligence Wiretap Court, which acts upon applications submitted to it by the Attorney General for leave to impose certain domestic wiretaps in the interest of national security.

Congress has created several other courts pursuant to its legislative powers under article I of the Constitution. Judges on these courts hold office for terms of years. These courts are usually referred to as legislative courts or article I courts. They function through procedures like those in article III courts; their business is judicial in nature, and they enter final judgments. They include the following:

- Court of Military Appeals. This court reviews court-martial convictions imposed in the armed services; its decisions are reviewable by the Supreme Court.

- Court of Veterans Appeals. This court reviews decisions of the Veterans Administration denying benefits claims by former members of the armed services; its decisions are subject to limited review in the U.S. Court of Appeals for the Federal Circuit.

- Tax Court. This court hears and decides claims by taxpayers against the federal government under the Internal Revenue Code; its decisions are reviewable by the courts of appeals in the geographical circuits.

- Claims Court. This court hears and decides monetary claims against the federal government; its decisions are reviewable by the U.S. Court of Appeals for the Federal Circuit.

- Bankruptcy Courts. These courts adjudicate a wide range of matters under the federal bankruptcy laws; their decisions are reviewable by either a district court or a court of appeals or by a special panel of bankruptcy judges.

The Business of the Federal Courts

The authority of the federal district courts, the major trial courts of the federal judicial system, is defined quite differently from that of the state trial courts. As explained in Chapter Two, state trial courts of general jurisdiction are open to entertain all types of legal disputes, regardless of the law under which they arise or the identity of the parties, unless they are specifically prohibited from doing so. By contrast, the federal district courts are not courts of general jurisdiction. They have authority to adjudicate only those types of cases specified in acts of Congress, and Congress can authorize them to entertain only the nine categories of "cases" and "controversies" listed in article III of the Constitution. Taken as a whole, these categories permit the federal trial courts to play an important role in the vindication of federal rights and in the resolution of interstate and international conflicts.

The major category of judicial business handled by the federal district courts consists of cases arising under federal law. These are cases in which the plaintiff's claim is based upon the Constitution or an act of Congress or a treaty. Most of the claims based upon the Constitution rely on the fourteenth amendment's due process and equal protection clauses. These cases are typically brought against state officials, state agencies, and city and county officials. Plaintiffs in such cases can seek damages or injunctions or both.

Suits arising under federal statutes form an increasingly significant portion of federal judicial business. Many of the regulatory statutes enacted by Congress in recent decades authorize individuals to sue for alleged violations. These statutes govern a wide range of concerns, including labor conditions, public accommodations, voting, safety, health, financial transactions, broadcasting, transportation, and environmental protection. In addition, older statutory provisions such as the antitrust laws give rise to much federal litigation. The statutes vary in the relief authorized. Under some the court can award only damages, under others only injunctions are available, and under still others both types of relief can be obtained. Although state law continues to govern a wide range of private transactions and the everyday affairs of most people, federal law has become increasingly pervasive, leaving few areas of life untouched. This means that the federal courts have a large and mixed array of cases based on the ever-growing body of federal statutory law.

The other major category of civil litigation in the federal district courts consists of "diversity" cases. District courts can adjudicate any civil action—regardless of the law under which the suit arises—in which citizens of different states are on opposing sides and the amount in controversy exceeds $50,000. There must be complete diversity of citizenship in multiparty cases; if citizens of the same state are found on both sides, the federal jurisdiction fails and the suit can be brought only in state court. Thus the federal courts can entertain all of the types of civil cases that the state courts can entertain—tort, contract, property, or whatever—so long as citizens of different states are opposing each other and more than $50,000 is involved. In almost all of these cases the governing law will be state law, and the federal district court will typically apply the law of the state in which it sits. There are only two exceptions to the rule of concurrent federal and state court jurisdiction in diversity cases: federal courts cannot hear domestic relations cases (e.g., divorce, child custody disputes) or cases involving the administration of deceased persons' estates.

Admiralty cases were one of the most important types of federal judicial business in the early days of the nation. This jurisdiction, inherited from the English courts, embraces all kinds of maritime claims involving navigable waters and shipping. Admiralty cases are still significant, but the quantity of such suits has diminished in proportion to the number of cases brought in other areas of federal jurisdiction.

All federal crimes must be prosecuted in the federal district courts. In the United States the basic protection of persons and property is a matter for state criminal law. Federal crimes (i.e., those crimes defined by act of Congress) relate to areas of special federal concern, such as interstate commerce, national security, and the federal government itself. The reach of federal authority in all of these areas has gradually expanded; federal crimes now include bank robbery, kidnapping, various drug-related activities, and fraud.

The business of the twelve geographically organized courts of appeals comes mainly by way of appeals from judgments of the district courts in their respective circuits. However, those appellate courts also have jurisdiction to entertain appeals of orders of certain federal administrative agencies. These include the National Labor Relations Board, the Securities and Exchange Commission, the Federal Trade Commission, and the Interstate Commerce Commission. Thus the courts of appeals decide all of the types of cases that the district courts decide, civil and criminal, and also review a wide array of administrative agency actions. Any of these cases that makes its way into a court of appeals can in turn be reviewed by the Supreme Court. A case over which the district courts have jurisdiction can thus go through three levels of the federal judiciary—from a district court to the court of appeals to the Supreme Court. Only a small fraction of district court cases, however, actually go beyond the courts of appeals. For practical purposes, and in the overwhelming majority of federal judicial business, the courts of appeals are the courts of last resort.

Cases that are initially filed in state trial courts can be taken into the federal courts in two ways. One is by way of removal at the outset. Subject to certain exceptions, if the case pending in the state court is one over which the federal district court also has jurisdiction, the defendant can remove it to the federal court. Thereafter that case proceeds through the federal system as though it had been filed in the federal court originally. This "removal jurisdiction" is said to provide an out-of-state defendant with protection against possible state court bias and to allow cases particularly suited for federal adjudication to be litigated from the outset in the federal system.

The other way a case filed in state court can enter the federal judicial system is through appellate review in the Supreme

Court after the case has been finally decided by the highest state court in which a decision could be had. This "highest court" is typically the state supreme court. As explained above, the Supreme Court has authority to review a state case only if the state court's decision involves a controlling question of federal law.

Federal and State Courts Compared

With its nationwide trial court base, the geographical expanse of the federal judiciary far exceeds that of any state judiciary. But apart from its territorial reach, the federal judicial system is no larger than that of some of the largest states. Indeed, in certain respects it is smaller than some of these state systems. Consider, for example, the total number of cases filed and appealed in a recent year in the courts of California, the most populous state, compared with case filings in all federal courts. The trial court figures are those relating to the federal district courts and to the California superior courts, that state's general jurisdiction courts. The figures are rounded to the nearest thousand, except for those of the supreme courts.

	California	Federal (Nationwide)
Trial Courts	944,000	279,000
Intermediate Appellate Courts	12,000	40,000
Supreme Court	3,200	4,917

These figures include all civil and criminal cases. Of course, filings do not necessarily reflect the judges' work burdens because many cases that are filed are later abandoned or settled without ever being acted on by a judge. Moreover, many filed cases are routine, such as uncontested divorces, requiring only slight judicial attention. Nevertheless, these figures do convey some sense of the volume of business flowing into these two court systems. It is interesting that while the volume of filings at the trial level in this one state far exceeds that of all federal district courts nationwide, the volume of appeals at the intermediate level in the federal system is more than three times the volume in the state system, suggesting that litigants in the federal district courts are more persistent and likely to press their cases on to the appellate level than are litigants in the California state courts. The filings in the U.S. Supreme Court include cases coming from the state supreme courts as well as from the lower federal courts, whereas the filings in the California Supreme Court come solely from that state's lower courts. The number of cases actually decided annually by both of these supreme courts is far less than the number of filings shown here because these courts exercise a discretionary jurisdiction and take for decision only a small percentage of filed cases.

Another comparison that can be made relates to the number of judges in these two judicial systems. The trial judges shown here are federal district judges and California superior court judges.

	California	Federal (Nationwide)
Trial Judges	725	632
Intermediate Appellate Judges	88	179
Supreme Court Justices	7	9
Total	820	820

While the total number of judges in these two systems is currently the same (a mere coincidence and subject to change as new judges are added in each system), the state judicial manpower is more heavily concentrated at the trial level. The greater number of intermediate appellate judges in the federal judiciary reflects the greater number of appeals received in that system.

In one other state, Illinois, where there is a unified trial court, the number of trial judges (760) exceeds the number of federal district judges. In states without a unified trial court, the great bulk of trial court work is done by the courts of limited jurisdiction. If the judges of these courts were taken into account, the trial judges in some states would outnumber those in the federal courts, even counting the non-article III federal magistrate judges and bankruptcy judges.

It should be underscored that a federal district court is a trial court essentially like a state trial court of general jurisdiction. Both types of courts function under substantially the same trial procedures. Indeed, in many states the trial court procedures are identical to those in the federal district courts. A casual observer of proceedings in a federal district court and a state trial court would notice few differences. In all large cities, as well as in many smaller towns, both courts are in session—often in courthouses within a few blocks of each other. From these two trial forums, however, the appellate routes diverge. An appeal in a federal case will go to the U.S. court of appeals for the circuit in which the trial court is located, a court embracing several states with its judges drawn from those states; the state case will go either to the state intermediate appellate court or the state supreme court, with judges drawn entirely from within that state.

Not only are the procedural rules and the adversary style of proceeding basically the same in the federal and state trial courts, but much of their business is also the same. Approximately one-fourth of the federal district court's civil docket consists of cases brought there under the diversity of citizenship jurisdiction, which means that they are essentially state law cases. In those cases the federal district courts are engaging in exactly the same kind of work as the state courts of general jurisdiction. In the rest of their business, however, both civil and criminal, the federal district courts are concerned primarily with issues of federal statutory law, intermingled with federal constitutional questions and maritime cases. Some of these questions also arise in state court litigation. In general, however, state courts are much more involved with the traditional common-law subjects than the federal courts, while the latter are much more heavily involved in adjudicating statutory and constitutional questions.

CHAPTER FOUR

COMPLICATING CIRCUMSTANCES

The extraordinary complications in the American legal order stem primarily from two circumstances. One is the existence in the United States of multiple sovereignties and hence multiple sources of law and multiple judicial systems. The other is the side-by-side existence of state and federal trial courts, with a substantial measure of overlapping jurisdiction. The situation is complicated still further by the mobility of American society and the regional or nationwide character of business and other human activities. These complicating factors will be discussed below.

Multiple Sovereignties: State-Federal and Multi-State

A great divide in the American legal order is that between state and federal law. In the federal sphere the Congress, executive departments, and administrative agencies are constantly generating laws and regulations. At the same time, in each of the fifty states the legislature, executive departments, and administrative agencies are also generating laws and regulations. Although state law continues to be the law governing the great bulk of everyday human activity, federal law has grown substantially in volume and coverage during the last half of the twentieth century. As indicated in the last chapter, federal law is now pervasive in American life, leaving few areas of human affairs wholly beyond its reach.

38

All persons and territory within the fifty states are subject to both federal and state law, with the exception of a few exclusively federal enclaves such as some military posts. Some matters are covered only by state law, while others are covered only by federal law. In still other instances both state and federal law apply to the same conduct. Sometimes federal and state laws are directed to the same end, so that either or both could be applied, albeit duplicatingly, to reach the same result.

In the criminal field, for example, robbery of a bank chartered under federal law is a federal crime. At the same time it is also a crime under state law. The offender could be prosecuted in federal court by federal authorities or in state court by state authorities. In this type of situation, executive policy or custom usually prescribes that one or the other sovereign should proceed with the case, but not both.

On the civil side many federal regulatory statutes concerning fiscal and commercial matters, as well as numerous other subjects, create a cause of action for persons injured in violation of these statutes. For many such activities state tort or commercial law also provides a cause of action. An injured person can choose to sue under either federal or state law.

One may wonder why Congress would enact laws, either civil or criminal, addressed to matters already covered by state law in a way that is consistent with Congressional thinking. There are at least two reasons. One is that the fifty state laws on the subject may not be, and usually are not, uniform. Congress could decide that the national interest requires that the particular activity be dealt with uniformly nationwide; only a federal statute can guarantee that. Another reason is that Congress may conclude that although state laws are adequate, there is need to bring federal resources to bear on the problems of enforcement. By bringing the field under federal law, cases arising in that area can be litigated in federal courts, and criminal offenses can be investigated and prosecuted by federal officials.

In addition to the sizable array of federal statutes that overlap with state law, there are duplicating federal and state constitutional provisions. Many state constitutions contain provisions controlling state governmental activity that are identical to provisions in the Federal Constitution. For example, state constitutions often prohibit the same sorts of state official actions that are proscribed by the due process and equal protection clauses in the fourteenth amendment to the Federal Constitution. Assuming that the language in both constitutions is interpreted the same, as is frequently the case, applying either constitution leads to the same result.

In all of the situations just discussed, federal and state law are consistent; the two are in large measure duplicative. In other instances, however, state and federal law may conflict. For example, the law of a particular state may make certain behavior unlawful, e.g., some kinds of concerted labor activity, while statutes enacted by Congress make that activity lawful. When there is a conflict of this sort, federal law prevails by force of the supremacy clause of the Federal Constitution. In this circumstance federal statutes are said to "preempt" state law. Supreme Court interpretations of the Constitution, especially those of the commerce clause, have expanded the potential reach of Congressional power. However, Congress has not chosen to exercise that power over many of the activities within its authority. Those activities remain under the exclusive domain of state law as long as no federal statute is enacted on the subject. Thus Congress could preempt state law, but until it does so, state law, either statutory or constitutional, continues to be operative unless it conflicts with the Federal Constitution.

Whether state or federal law is to be applied in a particular case does not—or, at least in theory, should not—vary depending on the court in which litigation takes place. The substantive law to be applied is the same whether the litigation is in a state court or a federal court. As we have seen in the previous chapters, state courts entertain many cases based on federal statutes and constitutional provisions. In so doing, they look to federal law for the governing rules and doctrine. Federal courts decide many cases under the diversity of citizenship jurisdiction that arise entirely under state law, and they apply that state law just as the state court would if the case were in the state court.

There is a significant difference, however, in these situations. When a state court adjudicates a case based on a federal cause of action or decides a controlling question of federal law in any kind of case, the judgment in that case, after final decision in the state's highest court, can be reviewed by the U.S. Supreme Court. When, however, a federal court decides a state law question, the state supreme court has no authority to review that decision. State courts have no jurisdiction to review judgments of federal courts. The federal-state jurisdictional relationship is thus asymmetrical.

To overcome some of the undesirable consequences of having no state court review of federal court decisions on state law questions, many states have enacted statutes or rules of court authorizing the state supreme court to receive and decide state law questions certified to it by a federal court. Under this procedure a federal court that has before it a case containing an unclear state law issue may, in its discretion, certify the issue to the state supreme court. Pending decision by the state court, the case will remain on the federal court's docket. After receiving the state court's decision, the federal court will decide any remaining questions in the case and enter final judgment. There is no comparable procedure whereby a state court can certify an unclear federal law question to a federal court.

Selection of the appropriate law to be applied to a given transaction is not simply a matter of determining whether it is to be state or federal. The choice-of-law problem can be considerably more complicated than that. In addition to the federally generated law, the fifty states generate fifty bodies of state substantive law.

Thus even though it is clear that federal law does not apply in a case, there may still be a question as to which state's law applies.

If all parties to a state law case reside in the state in which the court is sitting and all events giving rise to the litigation took place in that state, there is normally no question as to the applicable law; the law of that state will be applied. But litigation increasingly involves persons and events touching more than one state. The mobility and fluidity of American society have resulted in many activities and transactions that spill across several states. Those situations can produce difficult questions regarding the proper state law to apply. These choice-of-law conundrums are generally dealt with in American law schools in a course called Conflict of Laws and sometimes in the course called Federal Courts.

Consider two examples. *X*, a resident of Virginia, is driving his car to Florida when he collides in South Carolina with a car driven by *Y*, a resident of Georgia. To which state's law will a court look to determine the rights and liabilities of *X* and *Y*?

Suppose that *A*, a California resident, enters into a contract with *B*, a Texas resident, under which *B* agrees to construct a house for *A* in New Mexico. *B* defaults in performance of the contract, and *A* sues to recover damages for breach. Which state's law will the court apply?

Several decades ago the answers to these questions would have been easier than they are now. The law of the place where the wrong occurred or the contract was made might once have governed, but that is no longer necessarily so. The law of conflicts has evolved so that today a court must evaluate a variety of factors, including the respective interests of the various states having some connection with the parties or the events. Indeed, a court may decide that the law of one state will apply as to liability and the law of another state as to damages.

In the two hypothetical cases above, whether the litigation takes place in a state court or in a federal court (as it could, under the diversity of citizenship jurisdiction), the choice of law should be the same. The federal court will apply the same law that would be applied by a state court in the state in which the federal court is sitting. The choice might vary, however, with the state in which suit is brought, because one state's choice-of-law doctrines are not always the same as those in other states. While there are some federal constitutional restraints on the states in this regard, there is still much leeway available. This tangled area of American law cannot be explored here in more detail without taking on the entire course in Conflict of Laws.

Choice-of-law problems are magnified because American law is rather liberal in permitting suit against a person or a corporation in more than one state. A person can be sued in his home state and any other state in which, while physically present there, he is served with process (given a summons to appear in court to defend the action). A corporation can be sued in the state of its incorporation and any other state in which it is carrying on a substantial amount of business. Although the fourteenth amendment's due process clause places some limits on the exercise of state judicial power over defendants who are neither present in the state nor served there, under Supreme Court interpretations the scope of a state's judicial power over absent defendants is quite broad. A nonresident person or an out-of-state corporation having "minimum contact" with a state, sometimes even a single, isolated contact, may be sued in that state on claims arising out of that contact. Thus, in the automobile collision described above, either party could be sued in South Carolina, where the collision occurred, as well as in his home state or any other state in which he happened to be present and served with process. In the contract case, the defendant could be sued in Texas and probably in California or New Mexico, depending on his contacts in those states. Inasmuch as states have differing choice-of-law rules, choice of state in which suit is brought can sometimes control choice of substantive law governing the rights and liabilities of the parties.

Regardless of the substantive law being applied, a court will normally apply its own rules of procedure. For example, in the automobile collision case described above, if suit were brought in a Virginia state court, that court would follow the Virginia rules of procedure even if it determined that South Carolina substantive law should govern. If suit were brought in a federal district court in any state, that court would apply the Federal Rules of Civil Procedure, which control in all federal district courts nationwide irrespective of what substantive law the court applies.

Coexisting State and Federal Trial Courts

Complications in the American judicial scene resulting from the multiplicity of sources of law and court systems are magnified by the coexistence of state and federal trial courts with a substantial amount of duplicating authority. No other federalism in the world has a comprehensive set of federal trial courts functioning alongside state trial courts. In other federalisms the trial courts, with minor exceptions, are state courts; the only federal courts are appellate courts. In those systems there is thus no uncertainty about the proper court and no tactical decision to be made by plaintiffs and their counsel concerning whether to sue in state or federal court; all suits are initiated in state trial courts, and there is access to federal courts only by way of appeal. In those federalisms, because there are no side-by-side federal and state trial courts, there is no possibility of federal-state judicial conflict at the trial level.

By contrast, at any place in the United States there are always two trial courts sitting: a state trial court of general jurisdiction and a federal district court. That circumstance might not be troubling if each court's jurisdiction were exclusive of the other's. But that is not always the situation. In many instances, as has been noted, there is concurrent state and federal jurisdiction, so a plaintiff has a choice of forum. This concurrent jurisdiction gives federal district courts potential authority to interfere with state court proceedings by enjoining state court litigants. On the other hand, with a minor exception, state courts are without authority to enjoin litigants from proceeding in federal courts.

The judicial complexities of American federalism are so numerous that they cannot all be identified here or described in detail. A few should have become apparent from what has been said in the preceding pages. All that can be done here is to attempt to impart further the nature and extent of these complexities by giving some illustrations.

Assume that a large retail mercantile business in Pennsylvania orders products from a manufacturing business in Ohio. Thereafter a controversy erupts between the two over the quality of the products or the date of delivery. The retailer wishes to sue the manufacturer. It has four choices of forum. It can sue in a state trial court in Pennsylvania or a state trial court in Ohio, or it can sue in a federal district court in either state (assuming that more than $50,000 is involved).

If suit is brought in a Pennsylvania state trial court, there is a substantial likelihood that the court will apply Pennsylvania substantive law; courts tend to prefer to apply their own law where, as here, that is a plausible choice. The appeal in the case would go to the Pennsylvania intermediate appellate court, with the possibility of further review in the Pennsylvania Supreme Court. On the other hand, if the retailer sues in an Ohio state trial court, there is an equal likelihood that the court will apply Ohio law. The appeal would go to the Ohio intermediate appellate court, with the possibility of further review in the Ohio Supreme Court.

Although this is complicated enough, it is only half the story. Because the parties are of diverse state citizenship, the retailer could sue in a federal court in either of the two states involved. If suit were brought in a federal district court in Pennsylvania, that court should apply the same substantive law that the Pennsylvania state court would apply. The appeal would go to the U.S. Court of Appeals for the Third Circuit (embracing Pennsylvania and two other states). If Pennsylvania law were not clear, the court would make the best judgment it could as to what the Pennsylvania Supreme Court would do if it had that particular question before it. If the federal court erred, there would be no way for the state court to correct it.

If suit were instead filed in a federal court in Ohio, that court would apply the law that the Ohio state trial court would apply if the case had been brought there. Unlike Pennsylvania, Ohio has a rule authorizing its supreme court to receive and answer questions of state law certified to it by a federal court. Thus if Ohio law were not clear, the federal district court could invoke the certification procedure and receive a definite answer from the Ohio Supreme Court. The appeal would go to the U.S. Court of Appeals for the Sixth Circuit (embracing Ohio and three other states). If the district court had not certified the state law question to the Ohio Supreme Court, the court of appeals could do so.

In each of these federal suits, the U.S. Supreme Court would have jurisdiction to review the decision of the court of appeals. However, the Supreme Court almost never exercises its discretionary jurisdiction to review lower federal court decisions on state law questions.

It could be that Pennsylvania and Ohio law are identical as to the matters in dispute, so that as far as the substantive rules are concerned, the state in which the litigation takes place would make no difference. This would be a happy coincidence, however, for each state is empowered as a sovereign to fashion its law as it wishes, subject only to such constraints as may be imposed by the Federal Constitution.

Suppose now that the suit by the Pennsylvania retailer against the Ohio manufacturer was based not on state law but on a federal statute. Unless Congress had made federal jurisdiction exclusive, the plaintiff would have the same four-way choice of forum. Whether suit were brought in a state court in Pennsylvania or Ohio, the state supreme court's decision on the federal question would be reviewable by the U.S. Supreme Court.

If suit were brought in the federal district court in Pennsylvania, the appeal, as pointed out above, would be to the Third Circuit, whereas a suit filed in the federal district court in Ohio would take the appeal to the Sixth Circuit. These two federal appellate courts should in theory both give the same meaning to the federal statute and thus reach the same result. But in practice that does not always happen. Federal appellate courts sometimes reach different conclusions as to the meaning of a federal statute or constitutional provision. A federal appellate court in one circuit is not bound to follow a decision of a federal appellate court in another circuit. If the Sixth Circuit in a previous case had decided the same federal statutory question, the Third Circuit in this case could reach a different decision. In other words, the meaning of a federal law could be different in Pennsylvania from what it is in Ohio. When such an intercircuit conflict has occurred—that is, when one court of appeals has decided an issue of federal law in conflict with a decision of another court of appeals—the Supreme Court can grant certiorari and resolve the conflict. The Supreme Court can likewise resolve a conflict between two state supreme courts on a federal law question. The Supreme Court is thus a mechanism—the only judicial mechanism—for maintaining nation-wide uniformity in federal law. As a practical matter, however, the federal appellate courts and the state supreme courts annually decide such a huge number of cases that the Supreme Court has difficulty in resolving all conflicting decisions. This is one of numerous deficiencies in American judicial arrangements that needs correcting.

There are still other twists and complications to the case just hypothesized. If the Pennsylvania retailer sues the Ohio manufacturer in a Pennsylvania state court, the Ohio defendant can remove the case to the federal district court sitting in Pennsylvania. However, it could not remove the case to the federal court if the suit were brought in Ohio, because a defendant sued on a state law claim is not allowed to remove a case brought in a state court in his home state.

When a case is in a federal district court, whether it was filed there originally or removed from a state court, the federal court has authority to transfer it to another federal district if that court is one in which the plaintiff could have brought the suit initially. Thus, in the case above, if the suit were pending in the federal court in Pennsylvania, the court could, as a matter of discretion, transfer it to a federal court in Ohio if the court found that such a transfer was convenient for parties and witnesses and in the interest of justice. Such a transfer would, in this case, mean that the litigants were not only getting another trial forum but were also getting a different appellate court to which any appeal would be taken, as this transfer would take the case from the Third Circuit to the Sixth. However, if state law governed the case, it would not change with the transfer, as the court in Ohio would be required to apply the state law that would have been applied in the Pennsylvania court from which the case was transferred.

Shifting now to an entirely different situation, assume that a prosecution for a state crime is commenced in a state trial court. The defendant contends that the statute on which it is based violates some provision of the Federal Constitution, such as the equal protection clause or the first amendment. On that ground the defendant files suit in federal court to enjoin the state prosecutor from proceeding. The appropriateness of the federal court's granting relief in such circumstances has fluctuated over time. There has always been a special sensitivity about federal trial courts' interfering with the state criminal process. This sensitivity underlies a variety of the "abstention doctrines." Under these doctrines, developed in Supreme Court decisions, federal judges may decline to adjudicate certain cases out of respect for state court processes. As matters now stand, the federal court should enjoin the state prosecution only if it is brought in bad faith. However, if the federal action had been initiated before the state prosecution was actually launched, the federal court could grant relief to the potential defendant if the federal court found the state statute to be unconstitutional.

If the federal district court declines to grant relief in this situation, such action does not deprive the defendant altogether of access to a federal court. There are two additional opportunities available to him later. If he is convicted, and the conviction is affirmed by the state supreme court, he may petition the U.S. Supreme Court for certiorari. That Court could then, in its discretion, take up the case for decision and reverse the conviction if it found a violation of the Federal Constitution. If the defendant does not seek certiorari, or if the Supreme Court denies it, he can seek review by habeas corpus in a federal district court. The district courts have jurisdiction to issue writs of habeas corpus to review a deprivation of liberty when the petitioner contends that the restraint is in violation of the Federal Constitution. The Supreme Court has interpreted this jurisdiction to extend to custody under the judgment of a state court. Thus a state defendant who raises a constitutional objection during his trial can have that objection adjudicated later in a federal district court. In other words, the federal question in the case can be reviewed either by the Supreme Court directly or by a federal district court collaterally. In certain limited circumstances, a defendant may obtain collateral review of a state conviction even if he did not raise the federal question during the state trial. In a civil action brought in a state court there is no such collateral review available for federal questions; there is only direct Supreme Court review.

Outside the criminal field there are numerous situations in which a person may file suit in a federal district court against state officials, contending that they are acting in violation of the Federal Constitution. The relief usually sought is a declaratory judgment or injunction. For example, a corporation might assert that the state administrative agency charged with regulating corporations has issued a regulation that violates the due process clause in the fourteenth amendment. Such a regulation might also violate a similar provision in the state constitution. In that situation, the federal court could stay its hand to permit the plaintiff to get a determination in the state court of the state constitutional issue. If the regulation is indeed held invalid on state grounds, the federal court would not need to proceed further. This is another example of the application of one of the abstention doctrines.

The foregoing illustrations are but a few samples of the many, often subtle, interplays and potential conflicts between federal district courts and state trial courts. The full range of such instances is typically explored in American law schools in the course entitled Federal Courts and, to some extent, in the course on Civil Procedure and in other procedural courses. All of these problems stem from the side-by-side existence of state and federal trial courts throughout the nation with a considerable amount of overlapping jurisdiction, a circumstance, as pointed out above, unique to American federalism.

Complex Litigation

The American judicial scene has become still more complicated by the appearance, in the latter half of the twentieth century, of what is referred to as "complex litigation." This term is applied to controversies that are significantly different in size, scope, and difficulty from the bulk of civil cases that traditionally have filled the dockets of American courts. In those traditional cases one or a few plaintiffs sue one or a few defendants on one or a few claims. Factual and legal issues can be identified with relative ease, and the trial procedure can be focused on their resolution. A single final judgment can usually be entered for or against the plaintiffs, thus concluding the matter, subject only to appeal. Such cases still account for most trial court business, especially in the state courts, but civil litigation has become increasingly complex.

There are several varieties of complex litigation. One involves a single event—a major disaster such as a commercial airplane crash or a large hotel fire. Sometimes referred to as a "mass tort," an event of this kind can kill or injure hundreds of people. Each injured person and estate of a deceased person may have a claim against several defendants.

In a commercial airplane crash, for example, as many as three or four hundred passengers or their estates might assert claims against the airline for negligent operations, against various manufacturers of allegedly defective equipment (such as the engines, fuselage, or navigational system), and against the government or the airport for faulty flight control. The plaintiffs are likely to be residents of many states; the defendants are likely to be subject to suit in numerous states. Thus litigation is possible and indeed probable all across the nation. Each defendant could be subject to hundreds of suits in two or three dozen states. In each of these suits the issues as to the defendants' liability would be the same. However, the amount of damages to each plaintiff would vary. Some of these cases would be filed in state courts; others would be filed in federal courts. As to those in federal courts, it might be possible to consolidate them into one federal district through the transfer powers authorized by statute. But at present there is no way to gather into one forum cases in the courts of different states.

Another type of mass tort arises out of the defective manufacture of a product, such as a drug sold for medicinal purposes or a crucial part used in the manufacture of automobiles. Thousands of persons could be injured through the use of such a flawed product. But unlike injuries resulting from a single event, these injuries could occur over a period of years, at many different times and places. While in the single-event mass tort it is sometimes possible in the federal courts to gather many of the cases together and resolve them through a single proceeding, in this kind of widely dispersed harm consolidation may not be feasible because injuries may continue to occur after the disposal of some of the suits. The defendants are faced with potentially thousands of claims from unknown claimants over an indefinite period of time. The prospect of repetitive litigation is enormous because the issue of a defendant's liability will be essentially the same in all the cases.

In the commercial and financial fields there can also be mass wrongs. These typically occur when a large corporation or a stockbroker allegedly defrauds its stockholders or customers. Hundreds of thousands of persons could be cheated by illegal conduct of that sort, although the loss to each might be quite small. A multitude of individual suits could be filed in many state and federal courts, but here a class action may be available. Under this procedure some injured persons can sue as representatives of all. With the class as plaintiff, the entire controversy can be litigated in one proceeding in one court. There can still be plenty of procedural complications, however, especially problems of managing such a mammoth lawsuit. The judicial process, developed to govern the traditional kind of lawsuit, is not well adapted to resolving these mass claim situations.

A distinctively different type of complex litigation is produced by actions challenging the legality of the operation of large public institutions cr programs such as schools, mental hospitals, prisons, and welfare systems. Most such cases are brought in the federal district courts. Plaintiffs typically claim that the institution or program is being operated by state authorities in violation of some provision of the Federal Constitution. The relief sought usually cannot be accorded by a single judgment ordering the defendants to do or cease doing something specific. If plaintiffs have a well-founded claim, relief will often entail a substantial overhauling of the operations of the institution. Such relief will usually involve continuing supervision by the court over a protracted period of time, calling for substantial expenditures of public funds by the state. These types of cases have been referred to variously as institutional litigation, extended impact cases, and public law litigation. As with the mass claimant cases described above, the traditional judicial process is poorly adapted to cope with this sort of sprawling, multifaceted controversy. In addition, these cases give rise to special political sensitivities in that they put federal judges in the position of ordering state officials to change the ways in which they operate important state institutions and often, in effect, requiring state legislatures to appropriate funds for this purpose.

In numbers and in percentages, complex cases of all sorts occupy only a small part of the dockets of American trial courts. Yet they have an impact much greater than their numbers suggest in both their significance and in the resources they consume. These cases usually involve platoons of lawyers for the parties, large investments of judicial time, and often intractable problems of judicial management and supervision. The development of techniques (or alternative methods of dispute resolution) to manage these gargantuan controversies in a coherent and reasonably efficient way is one of the largest challenges facing American trial courts today.

CHAPTER FIVE

DRAMATIS PERSONAE

The multitudinous judicial systems in the United States are operated by a variety of persons. Judges are, of course, at the core of any court system. They are the decision makers, the key officials around whom all else is arranged. However, there is a vast supporting cast. Most intimately connected with the judges are those who assist them in the process of deciding issues and cases: law clerks, staff attorneys, and trial court adjuncts. Beyond these are the clerical and administrative personnel: secretaries, clerks of court and their staffs, judicial educators, and court administrators. Outside the court systems are numerous organizations whose functions are to assist the courts in various ways. Finally, there are the lawyers who present cases, thus supplying the grist for the judicial mill. The roles of all these persons and entities are described below.

Judges

Because American judges sit on courts of widely varying types and come from a variety of backgrounds and experiences, it is difficult to generalize about them. Two generalizations, however, are possible. First, judges in the United States initially come to the bench from other lines of legal work and after a substantial number of years of professional experience. Second, once on the bench they do not, in the main, follow a promotional pattern through the ranks of the judiciary. In these respects American judges differ from judges of the common-law and civil-law systems in other parts of the world.

In England, the legal ancestor of the United States, judges are likewise drawn from the experienced practitioners—barristers who have demonstrated competence in litigation. To that extent English judges resemble many American judges. But contrary to American practice, a barrister always enters the judiciary at the lower trial level. He is thereafter promoted, if he proves successful in the initial judicial post, first to the position of trial judge on the High Court, then possibly to the Court of Appeal, and then possibly to the highest court, the House of Lords. In other words, every judge on the High Court has served as a judge on a lower trial court, every judge on the Court of Appeal has served as a judge on the High Court, and every judge in the House of Lords has served as a judge on the Court of Appeal.

In the civil-law systems of Western Europe and of other parts of the world, in contrast to both England and the United States, the judges begin their professional careers as judges. They qualify to enter the judicial service after completing university law study and usually a short period of practical training. Having been appointed judges at the beginning of their legal careers, they are then promoted through the several higher levels of the judiciary. In this respect they resemble the English judges. The English judiciary combines the promotional feature of the civil-law system with the American practice of selecting judges from among experienced lawyers.

Compared to the English and civil-law systems of judicial recruitment and promotion, the methods used in the United States are quite varied. These procedures generally lack means of assuring professional quality. Moreover, the American judges' backgrounds are much more diverse than those of the English and civil-law judges. With the relatively minor exception of some lay judges on state courts of limited jurisdiction, all American judges have studied law and been licensed to practice law.

Although most judges have actually practiced law, the nature of that practice can be quite varied. Many judges have been litigators, but some have been office lawyers or counsel to organizations such as corporations or private associations. The types of law practice that judges have experienced range from small-town general practice to specialized fields in large metropolitan firms. Numerous judges have been lawyers in government service as prosecuting attorneys or counsel to government agencies, either state or federal. Some judges are former law professors, but their number is small. Many judges have earlier been active in political affairs, often as legislators, political campaign managers, or party committee members or chairmen. Indeed, many American judges can be described as former lawyer-politicians.

Another feature of the American judiciary that sharply distinguishes it from that of civil-law countries and other common-law countries is that persons can enter the judicial system at any level. A lawyer can initially become a judge on the highest court, the lowest court, or any court in between. There is no system or pattern about this. In other words, a lawyer who has never been a judge can become a judge on a court of last resort or an intermediate appellate court or a trial court, in either a state or the federal system. Lawyers who come on the bench at the trial or intermediate appellate levels have no real promise of moving to a higher court, although some may have hopes in that regard. Some judges do move up, but most spend their entire judicial careers on the same court. There is no system of promotion and no substantial sentiment among American lawyers, judges, or politicians that such a system would be desirable. There is, however, a body of opinion to the contrary. Views about judicial promotion vary from state to state. In Virginia, for example, there is a tradition of moving trial judges to the appellate bench, but in most states there is no such tradition. In the last decade or so it has been common for Presidents to nominate judges of appellate courts to be Justices on the U.S. Supreme Court, but that has not been the dominant pattern historically.

Lawyers become judges in the United States through four methods: (1) by nomination of the chief executive with confirmation by a legislative body, (2) by appointment of the chief executive from a short list of persons certified by an independent commission to be qualified for the position, (3) by popular election, and (4) by election in the legislature. Terms of office vary considerably from one system to another. They range from terms of years—some as short as four or six and a few as long as twelve to fifteen—to "good behavior," usually spoken of as a term "for life."

The federal system is the best known example of executive nomination with legislative confirmation. All federal judgeships are filled in this manner. The filling of district judgeships usually involves a significant amount of participation by members of the Senate, the confirming body. Senators view district judgeships in their states as being of special importance to them and their supporters. The Attorney General of the United States and the Department of Justice, which he heads, are key executive branch participants in the selection process, along with the White House staff. All of these participants must discuss and often negotiate with each other in order to arrive at a mutually agreeable choice—a person acceptable to them both professionally and politically. While the President ultimately selects the nominee, he is constrained as a practical matter by all these forces.

In making nominations for the U.S. courts of appeals the President and the Department of Justice have a somewhat freer hand, with less involvement by the Senators. Judges on each of these courts are drawn from several states, so no Senator has as strong an interest in the vacancy as he usually does in a district court position in his own state. In selecting Supreme Court nominees, the President has even more leeway, but he still must take into account sentiment in the Senate, as that body has in effect a veto power over the nomination.

Only a handful of states employ a judicial selection method similar to the federal. In most states the commission nominating method is used for at least some courts. In some states all judges are appointed through this process. In others it is used only for appellate judges. In still others it is used only for trial judges in certain cities or counties.

This so-called "merit plan" involves the use of an independent nominating commission, typically consisting of nine to fifteen members, a mixture of lawyers, judges, and nonlawyers. Efforts are usually made to constitute the body in a nonpartisan way to diminish as much as possible the aura of partisan politics in the selection process. When a judicial vacancy occurs, the commission invites suggestions from the bar and the public as to suitable nominees. It also receives applications from interested lawyers. The commission will then review all available information about each prospect and will often interview those who appear most promising. In the end it will submit to the Governor a list of those it considers best qualified, supposedly without regard to political affiliation. In some states the list consists of three names; in other states as many as five names may be submitted. From this list the Governor makes the appointment.

Often known as the "Missouri Plan" because it was first used in that state in 1940, this system is praised for providing a buffer against pure partisan politics, giving some assurance that judges will possess the requisite character and solid professional qualifications, and, at the same time, allowing leeway to the chief executive to make a choice, taking into account his policy judgments.

Despite the spread of this commission nominating system in the last half of the twentieth century and the continual campaign in its support, many states still choose judges at popular elections. This method of judicial selection, unknown in England and in the first decades of the United States, was introduced during the presidency of Andrew Jackson as an aspect of "Jacksonian democracy." In some states candidates for judgeships run under party labels like candidates for all other offices. In others they are on the ballot without party identification. Running for a judgeship under either arrangement raises special problems. A candidate for judicial office cannot have a "platform" or an agenda for action. The nature of the office requires that its holder be objective and above all that he not take a position in advance on any issue; judges must decide cases on the basis of the facts and the law as they appear when the case is before them for decision. That being so, there is little of significance that a judicial candidate can appropriately say. Another major problem is campaign financing. Campaigns for judgeships have become increasingly expensive, a condition exacerbated by the high cost of television advertising, considered essential to a successful race. The candidate must raise these funds from others, chiefly lawyers who will be appearing before him in the future. The damage to judicial objectivity and to the appearance of objectivity is obvious.

At the time of the formation of the Union, over half of the states chose their judges by election in the legislature. Now only two states employ this method, Virginia and South Carolina. While legislative election has disadvantages in that the decision often turns on partisan political factors, it has an advantage over popular election in that it does not involve extensive and costly campaigning by the prospective judge.

It is interesting that in many states where the law provides for the election of judges, the majority of judges are in fact appointed by the Governor. This is because the Governor is authorized to fill vacancies that occur between elections or legislative sessions, and many vacancies come about at those times through death, resignation, or retirement.

The concept of judicial independence, deriving in the United States from the separation of powers, means that in deciding cases judges are free from control by the executive and legislative branches of government as well as from control by the popular will of the moment. In other words, judges act free of extrajudicial controls in determining the facts, ascertaining and enunciating the law, and applying the law to the facts to arrive at decisions of cases. Although this concept is widely believed in and supported in the United States, it does not mean, and has never meant, an absolute and complete independence of the judiciary. That would not be tolerable in a democracy. Under democratic theory the people are sovereign. The judiciary, like the rest of government, must be ultimately accountable to the people. However, too much accountability can unduly impair independence. The tension between judicial independence and accountability cannot be altogether resolved. What one finds among the American judicial systems, therefore, are varying degrees of independence. The key element is tenure of office.

The highest degree of judicial independence is found in the federal system. All federal judges hold office during good behavior and can be removed only through impeachment by Congress. In an impeachment proceeding the House of Representatives must prefer charges against the judge by a majority vote, and the Senate must try the judge on those charges. The judge can be removed only if the Senate finds him guilty by a two-thirds vote. Impeachment is a formidable procedure, not easily invoked.

At the other end of the spectrum, affording the smallest degree of independence, are those state judicial systems in which judges hold office for terms of years, at the end of which they must stand for reelection by the voters. A judge with a term as short as four or six years, no matter how conscientious he may be, can hardly be unaware that his judicial decisions could become a political issue in the next election, never more than a few years away. Even if the judge himself can perform judicial duties without regard to such considerations, public suspicion of political influence will be a lurking threat to the appearance of justice. Short terms of office and popular election seem inconsistent with the concept of judicial independence. Yet such arrangements exist in many states along with praise for the virtues of judicial independence.

Judges whose terms are substantially longer are less likely to be influenced by political concerns. Longer terms also strengthen the appearance of judicial independence. Terms of twelve or fifteen years, found in some states, provide a higher degree of independence than terms of four or six years, but not as high a degree as tenure during good behavior. (Terms of state judges are shown in Appendix B.)

In some states the reelection of judges is by a "retention election." The judge runs on his own record without any opponent. The people are asked simply to vote "yes" or "no" on whether that judge shall be retained in office. That system works to afford a somewhat higher degree of independence than does a contested election. A judge knowing that he can be challenged by any lawyer who cares to pay the filing fee to become a candidate is likely to be more attentive to political currents and popular sentiment than a judge running only for retention on the record made.

Short terms and political elections are not the only threats to judicial independence. Independence can be impaired, or at least the appearance of independence damaged, in the process of executive appointments with legislative confirmation if the prospective appointee is required to indicate the positions he would take on legal issues likely to come before the court.

To sum up, long terms of office, difficult processes of removal, and protection against salary reductions are the principal elements that heighten judicial independence. Of great importance, however, are the customs and understandings relating to judges and their work. It is, for example, well-understood in the United States that it is improper for anyone to communicate with a judge concerning a pending case, other than the litigants and their lawyers acting through established procedural channels. It is universally acknowledged to be highly improper for anyone—a member of the legislature, an executive official, or a private citizen—to contact a judge in an effort to influence the judge's decision in any case. Such an action would be widely condemned, and, in fact, such improper contacts rarely occur. This deeply embedded understanding as to appropriate behavior in relation to the judiciary is itself a powerful protection of the judges' independence.

Law Clerks and Staff Attorneys

In the common-law tradition and in American practice prior to the twentieth century, judges functioned without assistance in judicial decision making. There has always been a clerk of court, a court employee who handles the papers and maintains case files. Judges also have long had secretarial help for typing and other clerical chores. But the judge alone, whether on the trial or appellate bench, did his own analysis of the legal issues and reached decisions unaided. If an opinion was to be written, the judge alone wrote it and verified the accuracy of all cited material. Yet by the middle of the twentieth century it was said, quite correctly, that the day of the unassisted judge had gone.

The first type of professional assistant to appear on the scene was the law clerk. Law clerks were introduced into the U.S. Supreme Court in the late nineteenth century and spread to the federal appellate courts in the 1920s. State supreme court judges then began to employ such assistants, and later they became standard in the state intermediate appellate courts. Some state trial judges have law clerks, but most do not. All federal district judges have law clerks.

All appellate judges, state and federal, now have at least one clerk each. Each U.S. Supreme Court Justice is allowed four; each U.S. court of appeals judge may have three. Most state supreme court justices have two clerks each; state intermediate court judges typically have one each, although some have more.

A law clerk is usually a recent law school graduate. For nearly all, a clerkship is the first job after graduation. Most clerks have strong academic records in law school. Many appellate judges require experience on a student-edited law school journal. Typically a clerk serves only one year, although some serve two. There are few career clerks.

The law clerk, sometimes called an "elbow clerk," is a personal assistant to the judge. The clerk's office or working area is usually immediately next to the judge's room, and there is frequent, daily contact. Judges use their clerks in various ways. In general clerks do legal research, prepare memoranda on the cases summarizing facts and issues and giving the clerk's analysis, edit drafts of opinions written by the judge, and serve as a sounding board and discussion partner for the judge. Work as a clerk is considered an excellent professional experience for a new law school graduate, a yearlong transition from the academic to the "real" world, with an opportunity to see the workings of the judicial process from the inside.

The work of law clerks in trial courts differs somewhat from that of law clerks in appellate courts. Appellate clerks spend much time in editing, and sometimes drafting, opinions that their judges are assigned to prepare for the court. Trial clerks also draft some memoranda and short opinions, but in addition they assist the judge with motions of all sorts and in pretrial conferences and hearings. They often deal directly with parties' lawyers to assist the judge in managing his docket. To a considerable extent these differing duties reflect the difference between the work of a trial court and that of an appellate court.

The idea of providing judges with law clerks and the growth in the number of clerks per judge have been the result of a continual rise in the volume of litigation. Beginning in the 1960s it became evident that appellate judges in particular needed and could effectively use still more professional help. Thus was developed the concept of central staff attorneys. Almost every state and federal appellate court of substantial size now has a central staff of lawyers.

The distinction between staff attorneys and law clerks is that the latter work for an individual judge in that judge's chambers; the relationship is direct and personal, with the clerk responsible to no one except that judge. Central staff attorneys, on the other hand, work for the court as a whole. Theirs is an institutional and not a personal responsibility.

Central staffs in appellate courts vary in size from two or three lawyers up to two or three dozen. Staffs often contain experienced lawyers who are making a career out of the job, along with recent law school graduates who are there for only a year or two. Typically a staff is headed by a career director who is responsible to the court for all staff work. Central staffs in appellate courts generally write memoranda on cases for the use of the judges to whom those cases are assigned. In some courts they also draft proposed dispositions, usually short opinions in cases with issues that are not especially difficult or novel.

Accompanying the introduction of central staffs into appellate courts, and also in response to the ever-rising volume of appeals, has been the adoption by those courts of screening and shortened internal procedures for deciding cases. Central staff attorneys often do the screening, a process of identifying those appeals that can appropriately be decided through truncated processes, usually involving the elimination of oral argument. These abbreviated processes can also include the disposition of cases by a brief written statement instead of a lengthy explanation. Such a statement is often called a "per curiam" opinion because it does not carry the name of an individual judge as its author.

When law clerks became common in appellate chambers, concern arose that the judges were unduly delegating to their clerks some aspects of the judicial role. Apprehensions intensified considerably with the introduction of central legal staffs. Unlike elbow clerks, who work closely with one judge, staff attorneys form an independent group of lawyers removed from close daily contact with judges. If appellate judges turn over to the staff responsibilities for screening, coupled with memorandum writing and opinion drafting, there is a distinct possibility that the judges could overly rely on the staff and simply approve its work without adequate review. With the high volume of appeals and the prospect of continued growth, it is unlikely that there will be any reduction in the numbers of law clerks and central staff attorneys employed in appellate courts. The best protection against inappropriate delegation of judicial authority, whether to law clerks or staff attorneys, is the conscientious dedication of each judge to his professional responsibility to understand the law and the facts in each case and to reach his own reasoned decisions.

Other Judicial Adjuncts

In Anglo-American legal systems at the trial level there is a type of judicial adjunct much older than law clerks and central staff attorneys. This is the "master" or "special master." This quasi-judicial position has long been used in various ways by American trial courts, state and federal.

A master's position is typically part-time, filled by court appointment on an ad hoc basis for a specific purpose. Masters are often practicing lawyers appointed to assist the court in particularly complicated or protracted matters. For example, in a civil action involving an elaborate financial accounting the trial judge might designate a lawyer as a master to conduct the accounting and report the results to the court. In cases requiring the testimony of numerous widely scattered witnesses, the court could appoint a master to preside over the taking of the testimony and to transmit that testimony to the court with recommendations for factual findings. Courts have also used masters in some complex cases; in public law litigation they assist in supervising implementation of decrees. Masters, however, are the exception and not the rule. They are adjuncts to the court and cannot be allowed to displace the judicial function—those nondelegable tasks that only judges themselves can perform. Their actions are in the form of recommendations to the judges, who exercise the final decision-making authority.

In the federal district courts in recent years a new kind of judicial adjunct has blossomed. Created by Congress in 1968 and now officially designated a "federal magistrate judge," this is a full-time judicial office, although in some courts it is filled on a part-time basis. Unlike federal judges, magistrate judges are appointed by the court, and they hold office for terms of eight years, with the possibility of reappointment.

Federal magistrate judges perform two kinds of functions. First, they hold hearings on a variety of motions, such as motions seeking to control lawyers' conduct of discovery in civil cases, and make recommendations to the district judge as to the disposition. Assistance of this sort enables district judges to dispose of these matters without having to sit to conduct hearings themselves; they can simply accept the magistrates' recommendations. Magistrate judges also hold evidentiary hearings on prisoners' petitions challenging the legality of their convictions, and they recommend factual findings to the judge. Second, magistrate judges are authorized to conduct trials in civil cases and in criminal misdemeanor cases if the parties consent. In other words, the parties can choose to go to trial before a magistrate judge instead of a district judge. If the parties exercise this option, the magistrate judge is empowered to decide the case and enter final judgment in the name of the district court.

In many state trial courts there are adjuncts variously entitled commissioners, referees, and part-time judges. In some state appellate courts there are commissioners who assist the court much as staff attorneys do. Judicial adjuncts of all sorts have become increasingly important as the volume of litigation has continued to rise and the number of judges has not kept pace with growing caseloads.

Administrative and Clerical Staffs

The central figures in the judiciary, the judges and those professionals who assist them directly in the decision of cases, constitute only a small percentage of the total personnel in a judicial system. Many more persons are employed in the administrative and supporting services that are essential to the functioning of the courts. For example, in the Virginia court system there are approximately 3,500 employees, but only 332 are judges; the Arizona judiciary employs approximately 4,500 persons, of whom only 315 are judges.

The oldest position within the supporting staff is the clerk of court. Every court, whether trial or appellate, state or federal, has a clerk who has a staff. The clerk's offices range from two or three employees in the smallest courts to dozens of employees in the busiest metropolitan courts. Whatever their size and whatever the nature of the court, the clerk's office is the place where lawyers and litigants file pleadings, motions, and other papers in the cases brought in the court. The clerk's office keeps a file on each case and maintains the docket book and the official record of the court's actions in all of its cases. All matters that come before the judges flow first through the clerk's office. That office is the chief point of contact between the court and the lawyers, as well as the public. The personnel of that office work closely with the judges in setting cases for hearing or trial and in generally managing the court's docket to keep the cases moving. An effectively functioning clerk's office is essential to a smoothly functioning court.

A relatively new figure in the judicial branch is the court administrator. Almost unknown in American courts until the last third of the twentieth century, court administrators are now commonplace. A school has even been established to train persons for careers in this field: the Institute for Court Management in Denver, Colorado.

Every state has a state court administrator. This is the top administrative official in the statewide system, usually responsible directly to the chief justice of the state. The administrator assists the chief justice in a wide array of matters such as developing the annual budget for the state's court system, supervising non-judicial personnel, maintaining statistics on the state's judicial business, overseeing court buildings, and supplying equipment for the courts. State court administrators often have sizable staffs to carry out these responsibilities. In addition, the largest metropolitan trial courts frequently have their own court administrators. Those officials, under the direction of the chief judge, do for that particular court what the state court administrator does for the statewide system.

The federal judiciary has a central administrative office in Washington known as the Administrative Office of the United States Courts. It performs for the federal courts functions similar to those performed for state systems by the state court administrators and their offices. In addition, each of the federal judicial circuits has a circuit executive who serves as an administrative assistant to the chief judge of the circuit in managing the circuit's business.

Secretaries to judges are essential for the handling of the paper in the judges' chambers. Every appellate judge has a secretary, and some have two or more. Many trial judges have secretaries, but in some smaller courts and courts of limited jurisdiction a judge has only a part-time secretary or a secretary shared with another judge.

The newest type of administrative official, now found in every state judicial system, is the state judicial educator. This officer, who usually works under the direction of the state chief justice or a judicial council of some sort, is responsible for planning and carrying out programs of continuing education for the state's judges and other court personnel. These programs typically range from two or three days up to a week in duration. In most states such educational undertakings are offered for judges at all levels, most commonly for trial judges of the general and limited jurisdiction courts. These programs are part of a nationwide development in judicial education that will be described below.

In addition to all of these administrative and supporting personnel, there are battalions of others who help keep the courts running. These include bailiffs, computer operators, court stenographers, typists, guards, and building maintenance staffs. American court systems are now elaborate enterprises compared to the nineteenth-century courts, which often had only a judge, a clerk of court, and perhaps a bailiff. Yet courts are still relatively small compared with many bureaucracies in the executive branch of American government.

Supporting Organizations

All of the types of persons described above—judges, law clerks, central staff attorneys, judicial adjuncts, and administrative and clerical personnel—are employed within judicial systems. They make up the "third branch" of government in the state and federal spheres. But there are also many organizations and entities of various kinds outside the judicial branch that work with and offer support to the courts. These organizations are mainly private, although some have close governmental linkages. Collectively they form an important part of the American judicial scene and do much to strengthen the courts and enhance the quality of the administration of justice.

For the state judiciaries the most important of these is the National Center for State Courts, which has its headquarters in Williamsburg, Virginia. Established in 1971, the Center is supported by contributions from all fifty states and by grants from numerous sources. It provides advice and assistance to state courts regarding technological developments and procedural innovations. It collects statistical data on the personnel and caseloads of the state courts and generally acts as a clearinghouse for exchanges of information among the state courts. It also conducts research and publishes reports on a variety of state court problems.

Many small independent organizations, too numerous to list here, also carry out research on the functioning of courts. They often employ social scientists who conduct empirical studies on subjects such as the time consumed in adjudication and the relationship of certain procedures to expense and delay.

The State Justice Institute was created by Congress in 1986 to provide a conduit for channeling federal funds to assist the state courts. Although some federal money had gone indirectly to assist state courts in earlier years, the establishment of SJI was the first time that Congress had expressly recognized that there is a federal interest in the quality of state courts because those courts adjudicate the overwhelming number of disputes in the United States and also decide a significant number of federal law questions. With headquarters in Alexandria, Virginia, SJI makes grants annually from its congressional appropriation directly to the various state judicial systems and to the many entities assisting those systems. Judicial education has been a major beneficiary of its grants.

Several national organizations provide educational programs for state judges. The idea of continuing judicial education took root in the 1960s. The concept has now become widely accepted, and virtually every judge now regularly pursues such instruction. As mentioned in the last section, every state has its own judicial education programs. Beyond those, national programs, bringing together judges from many states, are offered through such organizations as the National Judicial College, the Institute for Court Management, the Institute of Judicial Administration, the American Academy of Judicial Education, the American Bar Association, and the American Judicature Society. A few university law schools offer short courses from time to time for judges. The most ambitious course of study is the Graduate Program for Judges at the University of Virginia School of Law. Begun in 1980 for appellate judges, it is the only course of study for judges conducted by a law school that leads to the award of a university degree. A similar program for trial judges, though not under the aegis of a law school, is conducted at the University of Nevada in collaboration with the National Judicial College.

The Federal Judicial Center, located in Washington, is an important supporting agency for the federal courts. Although established by Congress as an official part of the judicial branch, it has a substantial degree of autonomy. Its work falls into two divisions: research and education. Its professional staff conducts research and publishes reports on various aspects of federal judicial activity, with a view toward improving the federal judicial system. Its staff also plans and conducts educational programs for federal judges and other personnel within the federal judiciary.

The addresses of the supporting organizations mentioned here are set out in Appendix E.

Lawyers

It is a longstanding tradition in the Anglo-American legal world that anyone can represent himself in court. But contemporary law and judicial procedure are so complicated that it is unrealistic for a litigant to represent himself in any but the simplest matters. Lawyers are essential to ensure the full and fair presentation of cases. American courts, being passive agencies in the common-law tradition, depend on lawyers to present the litigants' positions and to develop the evidence and the legal arguments. Under the adversary system it is each lawyer's obligation to present his client's case to the court vigorously and completely. Lawyers are thus an integral part of the machinery of justice.

In the United States admission to the practice of law and the governance of the legal profession are matters of state concern. One can speak accurately, for example, of "the Virginia bar" or "the Texas bar" or "the Illinois bar," meaning the lawyers in each of those states who have been licensed by those states. There is no such thing as "the American bar" in any official or formal sense. That expression is used loosely to refer to all the lawyers in the United States, each of whom has been state-licensed. There is no national or federal authority to admit persons to the legal profession. The entity known as the American Bar Association is a private, voluntary, nationwide organization of some 370,000 lawyers from all states; it is the largest organization of lawyers in the country, although there are many other private bar associations, often based on areas of legal specialization.

In each state the requirements for admission to the bar are set by the supreme court or the legislature or the two acting together. Typically graduation from an accredited law school is required; there are more than 170 such schools in the United States, almost all affiliated with universities. Law school requires a three-year course of study after a student has attended college for four years and received a bachelor's degree. Law school graduates are awarded the degree of Juris Doctor (J.D.). They are then eligible to take a state bar examination, a written examination lasting two or three days. These examinations are usually administered by a body of lawyers, known as bar examiners, acting under the authority of the state's supreme court. Applicants who pass the bar examination and who also meet the requisite standards of character are admitted into the bar by that court.

Within the legal profession there is no formal division; there are no barristers or solicitors. Anyone admitted to the bar in a state is legally authorized to engage in any kind of legal practice in that state. As a practical matter, though, there is an increasing degree of specialization among lawyers. Typical areas of specialization are litigation, taxation, labor law, patent law, family law, trusts and estates, and various branches of administrative law.

A lawyer admitted to one state's bar can practice in another state only if he gets admitted in that state or that state recognizes the original state's admission. This kind of reciprocity is accorded in some states but not in all. However, a court may occasionally permit a lawyer from another state to appear before it for the purpose of presenting a particular case (*pro hac vice*) if there is some special reason for doing so.

In 1990 there were approximately 741,000 persons who were members of the bar in the United States, more than double the number in 1970. In addition to this large growth in numbers, the last ten to twenty years have brought extraordinary changes in the composition of the American legal profession and in the nature of law practice. The most striking change in composition has been the increase in the number of women. In 1980 they amounted to 8% of the bar nationwide; in 1990 they comprised approximately 22%.

A major change in the nature of practice has been in the growth of the large urban law firms. They have expanded enormously in the number of their partners and associates, and they have become national and international, each firm typically having offices in several American cities and, increasingly, in foreign cities. Many of these firms have hundreds of lawyers spread throughout their several offices, and sometimes a single office will have two or three hundred attorneys. Another significant change in the nature of practice, noted above, has been the increase in specialization among lawyers in both large and small firms.

As large and as publicized as they are, the giant metropolitan firms actually have in their ranks only a small percentage of the total number of American lawyers. A sizable percentage practice alone. Many others are in small firms ranging from two or three partners up to a dozen or more. A firm of thirty to fifty lawyers would now be considered middle-sized.

The total figure given above is misleading as to the number of actively practicing lawyers in the country. That figure includes every living person who has been admitted to the bar. Many of those persons are retired. Many do not engage in any legal work but pursue other careers, often in business. The figure also includes all those who are judges and law professors. Many lawyers are employed by government—federal, state, and local—in positions such as prosecuting attorneys, counsel to agencies, and staff attorneys in innumerable government departments and offices. Many other lawyers are "house counsel" in private corporations and other nongovernmental organizations; they work full-time exclusively for those employers. As all of this suggests, there is a varied and rich array of career paths open to American lawyers.

The independence of the bar is among the oldest and most deeply ingrained traditions in Anglo-American law. It means essentially that the lawyers are free from external control, except by the courts. The processes of admitting persons to the bar, of investigating complaints against lawyers, and of disciplining and disbarring lawyers are all administered by the bar itself or the highest court of the state or the two acting together. The bar's independence has always been deemed an important safeguard for individual liberty and protection against overweening governmental power. It leaves lawyers free to represent any clients they desire and to assert whatever legal positions they think necessary to protect their clients' interests.

Each state's bar is typically governed through the official statewide bar organization to which all the state's lawyers belong. This body is usually authorized by legislative enactment or supreme court rule to exercise control over admissions to practice and over disciplinary proceedings involving lawyers. Often the supreme court is given jurisdiction by the legislature over these matters, and it then delegates that authority to the state bar, reserving, however, the power to review the state bar's actions.

Two potential threats to the independence of the bar loom in the United States. One is the movement—much discussed but not very far advanced—to bring lawyers under the control of bodies consisting, at least in part, of nonlawyers. The argument for such external control is that the public has a substantial interest in policing the legal profession to ensure that its members do not defraud or mistreat persons they serve. The danger in this so-called public regulation of the bar is that lawyers could be subjected to restraints or punitive actions because of their representation of unpopular clients or because of partisan political considerations.

The other threat to lawyers' independence comes from the changed nature of law practice and from altered rules on professional conduct. Many lawyers today work for a single client or for a few similar clients; their livelihood is dependent on the satisfaction of those clients. Human nature being what it is, a lawyer in such a position is not as likely to exercise a high degree of truly independent judgment in giving advice as is a practitioner having numerous, diverse clients with no dependence on any one of them.

The rules of professional responsibility now permit advertising by lawyers, and this has tended to inject an increasingly commercial atmosphere into law practice. A lawyer who has affirmatively sought clients may be reluctant to give such clients legal advice that, albeit sound, would be unwelcome. The economic concern that prompted the lawyer to recruit clients through aggressive advertising is likely to make the lawyer shy away from advice that clients would not want to hear.

As is evident from the foregoing, a huge number of American lawyers are not involved with the courts; they spend their time in law offices, government bureaus, corporate buildings, conference rooms, and legislative halls. Only a relatively small number of practicing lawyers are actively engaged in litigation. Of those, many rarely appear in courtrooms. Civil litigation today, in contrast to that of several decades ago, consists in large measure of pretrial activity such as drafting pleadings and motions, examining documents, questioning witnesses on depositions, preparing and answering interrogatories, and participating in negotiations with other lawyers and in pretrial conferences with judges. In criminal cases much time is devoted to investigation, negotiations between prosecutors and defense counsel about charges and pleas, and the sentencing process.

Although precise figures are not available, it is clear that only a small minority of American lawyers appear frequently in trial courts to conduct trials or in appellate courts to present oral arguments. Yet that minority is the most visible slice of the legal profession. Those are the lawyers one is most likely to encounter in novels, motion pictures, and television programs. Known collectively as the "trial bar," they are the lawyers most intimately connected with the administration of justice. They form a vital part of the judicial machinery and directly affect, for better or worse, the quality and appearance of justice in the courts. In the United States, as in the common-law world generally, an independent trial bar combined with an independent judiciary is seen as powerful support for the rule of law and as a bulwark against tyranny. Thus it is considered to be of fundamental importance that these twin elements of American judicial systems be preserved amidst all the changes in law and society that are occurring and that will continue to occur.

Chapter Six

TRENDS AND DIRECTIONS

Magna Carta required the Court of Common Pleas to sit always in Westminster Hall. This seemingly trivial administrative provision in that seminal document in the development of English—and hence American—law and constitutionalism was pregnant with meaning and symbolism. For there in the year 1215 its drafters were saying that this law court should be located in what was then the largest and most important public building in the realm, a known, highly visible place where the court could always be found. That idea was carried across the Atlantic where it took root in hundreds of county seat towns stretching from the Eastern Seaboard to the Far West. As new settlements were created one of the first and most prominent structures to be erected was the courthouse.

Still today, if motorists leave the interstate highways and drive through the centers of the county seats from coast to coast, they will usually find the courthouse at the heart of town, the most impressive public building. Churches are usually there also, reflecting the reality that law and religion were central concerns of those who settled and built this country. Indeed, it has often been said that law is America's civic religion, one to which all of the diverse religious and cultural groups can give allegiance. Law, it has also been said, is the mortar that holds together the bricks of the heterogeneous American society.

77

In American courts, state and federal, the imprint of the English common-law process remains clearly visible in style, procedure, and substance. The continuity is impressive. The judge presiding over a trial in the clock-towered Victorian courthouse dominating the main street in Greenville, Alabama, and the Hawaii Supreme Court justices sitting in the Ali'iolani Hale, surrounded by the Pacific vastness, as well as thousands of other judges in American courthouses, function in a direct line of succession from the courts in Westminster Hall. A barrister plucked from those courts in the eighteenth century and miraculously transported to virtually any American courtroom today would not feel altogether a stranger.

And yet immense changes have taken place. The outpouring of legislation, state and federal, has already been mentioned. Moreover, American judges must cope with an ever-proliferating body of judicial decisions, precedents that must be followed. Increasingly, though, the judge and his law clerk will find those reported decisions on a computer screen rather than in bound books on shelves. Electronic data retrieval systems and other technological innovations have entered the world of the judiciary. Computers are used in court clerks' offices to maintain and manage dockets. Judges sometimes hold hearings through telephone conference calls, with the opposing lawyers and the judge all at different locations. Depositions of witnesses are often recorded on videotape, which can in turn be shown to a jury without the witnesses's presence at trial. Closed-circuit television can be used by an appellate court to hear oral argument, with the lawyers and the judges in different cities.

Although the adversary style still predominates in American courts, trial judges in the busiest courts, as mentioned in Chapter One, have increasingly come to take a more active role in managing litigation at the pretrial stage. This development, especially marked in the federal district courts, has modified the pure adversary process by placing the movement and shaping of cases to a considerable extent in judges' hands, thus reducing the traditional control of lawyers. The process is beginning to bear some resemblance to European civil-law procedures, under which the judge takes significant responsibility for moving the case along through a series of conferences and hearings. However, in the United States, the gathering and presentation of evidence and the development of the legal theories in the case remain the exclusive province of the advocates for the parties.

The pressures of litigation growth and the accompanying expense and delay have led not only to increased pretrial judicial management, but also to a search for means other than litigation for resolving some controversies. This search has led to the rise of the "alternative dispute resolution" movement, known for short as ADR. The movement is fed by three different but often overlapping concerns. One is concern about overloaded courts, coupled with the desire to reduce the quantity of judicial business. Another is a concern about the need for access to a process that is less expensive and burdensome than traditional litigation. Still another is concern that courts are not the best agencies for resolving certain types of controversies. The adversary process is seen as ill-suited to settling disputes when the parties are in ongoing relationships that they may wish to continue. Such relationships may involve members of a family, landlords and tenants, schools and students, or local merchants and customers. Whatever the motivation, the movement has caught on, and ADR programs have sprung up in all parts of the country.

One type of ADR involves the use of trained mediators who meet with the parties to the dispute and attempt to bring them together in a mutually agreeable solution. Another type involves arbitration, in which a third party hears informally from both parties and then renders a decision. "Court-annexed arbitration" has become popular. Under such a program, a court automatically refers certain cases to a panel of three arbitrators. Typically, these are cases in which only money damages up to a specified amount are sought. If either party is dissatisfied with the arbitrators' decision, he can restore the case to the court's docket and resume litigation. Other short, informal procedures are being experimented with in an effort to relieve court dockets, reduce delay and expense, and provide a dispute-resolving process that is more satisfying to the disputants.

In civil litigation one type of possible innovation is the establishment of different procedural tracks for different kinds of cases. This idea is fueled by the continuing growth in the variety, number, and complexity of cases and by the insights gained from experiences with affirmative case management and ADR. The idea runs counter to the predominant procedural gospel since the 1938 adoption of the pioneering Federal Rules of Civil Procedure. Those rules have been widely copied by the states, and today they represent the prevailing pattern of procedural rules in American trial courts. A major premise of those rules is that all civil cases should be governed by the same procedures, that there should be uniformity in civil practice regardless of the nature of the case. Now there is a growing body of opinion that such "trans-substantive" rules are not necessarily the fairest or the most efficient. The years ahead may bring the development of different sets of rules for different types of cases, supposedly tailored to the distinctive features of the subject matter. This has already happened to some extent in the federal courts, where there is a *Manual for Complex Litigation* suggesting procedures for the more complicated cases.

The wise allocation of judicial business between the state and federal courts has been a concern since the creation of the federal government in 1789. As already pointed out, there is much concurrent state and federal jurisdiction. Some of this is dysfunctional and should be eliminated. The diversity of citizenship jurisdiction of the federal district courts has been recurrently the object of controversy. The move to curtail it, thereby leaving state law cases entirely to the state courts, is gaining. At the same time there is an effort to enlarge the diversity jurisdiction to p̲ litigation in a federal court of cases with numerous and widely dispersed parties that cannot at present be litigated in any single forum. Another object of controversy is the federal courts' habeas corpus jurisdiction that enables those courts to review state criminal convictions. Efforts have been under way to contract this sort of collateral federal review, thereby according greater finality to state criminal processes. The relationships between state and federal courts and between state and federal law in these and other areas present the never-ending problem of striking a workable balance in the fair and effective administration of justice in this complicated American federalism.

Progress is being made toward developing a closer and more cooperative relationship between the state and federal courts. In some states federal-state judicial councils have been created. Each such body consists of the federal district judges in that state and selected state judges, including the state chief justice. They meet from time to time to discuss problems of mutual interest, such as those generated by federal habeas corpus review of state criminal cases. In April of 1990 the Federal Courts Study Committee, a high-ranking body created pursuant to an act of Congress, recommended the establishment of a national federal-state judicial council, consisting of federal and state judges, to work on problems of nationwide interest.

The continued growth in the volume of cases, civil and criminal, will present challenges to all American judicial systems. Structures, procedures, and personnel will probably undergo further changes. The number of judges will continue to increase. There may also be increases in the number of professional assistants for judges, thereby heightening concern about improper delegation of judicial authority. Differentiated procedures and innovative ways of processing cases will be pursued in both trial and appellate courts.

In particular, complex litigation involving large numbers of parties suing in many different states has spurred a search for devices to coordinate litigation and to gather it into a single forum. Proposals are being studied by Congress, the American Bar Association, and the American Law Institute. Efforts such as these should lead eventually to closer and more rational connections between state and federal courts. The proposals under consideration would provide for transfers of cases more readily from one federal court to another, as well as among state courts. They would also provide much wider ranging possibilities for removal of cases from state courts to federal courts and would, for the first time, provide means of transferring cases from federal courts to state courts. All of this has the objective of gathering into a single forum numerous and widely dispersed cases arising out of the same events. Achieving that end will be difficult, however, because of conflicting considerations involving efficiency, economy, fairness, and litigant autonomy. But if procedures of this sort can be developed and sufficiently refined, the hundreds of state and federal trial courts all across the nation could become one integrated network of forums among which cases could be moved and consolidated, as the circumstances required, to avoid a multiplicity of suits with potentially inconsistent results. If taken far enough, these developments could erode the significance of state boundaries and of the jurisdictional lines between state and federal courts.

Whatever may or may not happen in those directions, pressures on the appellate courts are likely to become especially acute. As appeals increase, more and more panels of judges will be necessary at the intermediate appellate level. This in turn will increase the likelihood of conflicting or nonuniform decisions at that level. At the same time there will continue to be the single court of last resort, increasingly unable to monitor the ever-swelling stream of decisions from the multiple intermediate panels. The pressures will be especially intense in the most populous states and in the federal system. In the latter it is already a concern of some magnitude; the U.S. Supreme Court is the sole court empowered to review decisions of the thirteen federal courts of appeals and the supreme courts of all the states in an effort to maintain nationwide uniformity in federal law.

Although there is much continuity with the past among American courts in their structure, procedure, and the nature of their business, many changes have taken place in the last third of the twentieth century, and more are in the offing. Greater attention than ever before is being given to planning for the future of the judiciary. Several states have created "Commissions on the Future of the Courts," and the Federal Courts Study Committee's report of April 1990 recommended that a long-range planning entity be created for the federal judiciary. In May 1990 a national conference on the future and the courts attracted several hundred judges, lawyers, and others from state and federal jurisdictions all across the country. A variety of trends and changes at work in American society will have a significant impact on the courts. These include intensified environmental difficulties, alterations in family structures, a growing heterogeneousness culturally and ethnically, and increasing internationalization of life. It is extremely difficult to predict the effects on the courts of these and other events. Nevertheless, many judges, lawyers, and students of the courts predict a continued movement away from the formal judicial process of adversary litigation toward various alternative dispute resolution procedures that are less confrontational. Technological developments are expected to play an increasing role in the workings of courts. Also anticipated is an integrated national network of courts in which the various state court systems and the federal system will be drawn closer together in the management of the nation's judicial business. Whatever changes lie ahead—and most of them cannot be accurately foreseen— American courts will likely remain the major institutions for the adjudication of serious disputes, as well as the ultimate backup systems when other means fail. In any event, amidst the complications of American federalism, the state and federal courts will almost surely continue as the institutions that give life to and symbolize the rule of law.

ILLUSTRATIVE STATE JUDICIAL STRUCTURES

California
Georgia
Illinois
Iowa
Virginia

The diagrams included here are adapted from those contained in *State Court Caseload Statistics: Annual Report 1988*, published by the National Center for State Courts.

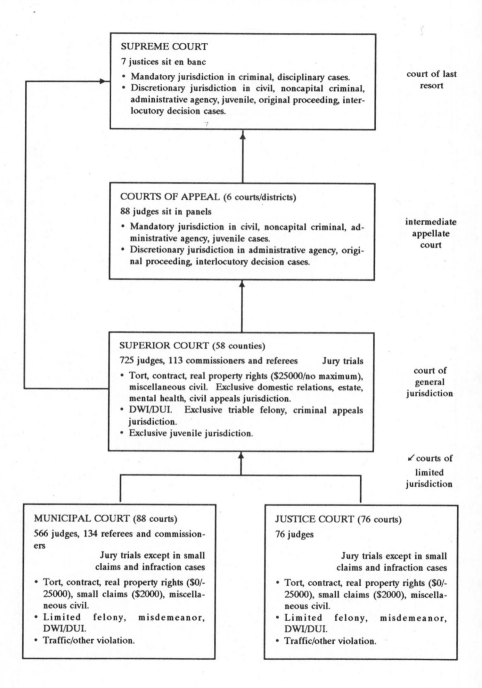

SUPREME COURT

7 justices sit en banc

- Mandatory jurisdiction in criminal, disciplinary cases.
- Discretionary jurisdiction in civil, noncapital criminal, administrative agency, juvenile, original proceeding, interlocutory decision cases.

court of last resort

COURTS OF APPEAL (6 courts/districts)

88 judges sit in panels

- Mandatory jurisdiction in civil, noncapital criminal, administrative agency, juvenile cases.
- Discretionary jurisdiction in administrative agency, original proceeding, interlocutory decision cases.

intermediate appellate court

SUPERIOR COURT (58 counties)

725 judges, 113 commissioners and referees   Jury trials

- Tort, contract, real property rights ($25000/no maximum), miscellaneous civil. Exclusive domestic relations, estate, mental health, civil appeals jurisdiction.
- DWI/DUI. Exclusive triable felony, criminal appeals jurisdiction.
- Exclusive juvenile jurisdiction.

court of general jurisdiction

✓ courts of limited jurisdiction

MUNICIPAL COURT (88 courts)

566 judges, 134 referees and commissioners

Jury trials except in small claims and infraction cases

- Tort, contract, real property rights ($0/-25000), small claims ($2000), miscellaneous civil.
- Limited felony, misdemeanor, DWI/DUI.
- Traffic/other violation.

JUSTICE COURT (76 courts)

76 judges

Jury trials except in small claims and infraction cases

- Tort, contract, real property rights ($0/-25000), small claims ($2000), miscellaneous civil.
- Limited felony, misdemeanor, DWI/DUI.
- Traffic/other violation.

SUPREME COURT   7 justices sit en banc

- Mandatory jurisdiction in civil, criminal, administrative agency, juvenile, disciplinary, certified question from federal courts, original proceeding cases.
- Discretionary jurisdiction in civil, non-capital criminal, administrative agency, juvenile, original proceeding, interlocutory decision cases.

court
of last
resort

▲

COURT OF APPEALS   9 judges sit in panels and en banc

- Mandatory jurisdiction in civil, noncapital criminal, administrative agency, juvenile, original proceeding, interlocutory decision cases.
- Discretionary jurisdiction in civil, noncapital criminal, administrative agency, juvenile, original proceeding, interlocutory decision cases.

intermediate
appellate
court

▲

court of
←general
jurisdiction

SUPERIOR COURT (45 circuits among 159 counties)   137 judges

- Tort, contract, miscellaneous civil. Exclusive real property rights, domestic relations, civil appeals jurisdiction.
- Misdemeanor, DWI/DUI. Exclusive triable felony, criminal appeals.
- Traffic/other violation, except for parking.   Jury trials.

courts of
✓limited
jurisdiction

▲   ▲   ▲

CIVIL COURT (Bibb and Richmond counties) 3 judges

- Tort, contract ($0/7500-25000), small claims ($0/7500-25000).
- Limited felony. Jury trials

MUNICIPAL COURT (1 court in Columbus) 1 judge

- Tort, contract ($0/7500), small claims ($0/7500).
- Limited felony, misdemeanor.
  Jury trials in civil cases

STATE COURT (63 courts) 36 full-time and 48 part-time judges, and 2 associates

- Tort, contract, small claims, civil appeals, miscellaneous civil.
- Limited felony, misdemeanor, DWI/DUI.
- Moving traffic, miscellaneous traffic.   Jury trials

COUNTY RECORDERS COURT (Chatham, DeKalb, Gwinnett, and Muscogee counties) 8 judges

- Traffic/other violation.
- Limited felony, DWI/DUI.   No jury trials

MAGISTRATES COURT (159 counties) 159 chief magistrates and 267 magistrates, 36 of whom also serve State, Probate, Juvenile, Civil, or Municipal Courts.

- Tort, contract ($0/3000), small claims ($0/3000).
- Limited felony, limited misdemeanor.
- Ordinance violation.   No jury trials

PROBATE COURT (159 counties) 159 judges

- Mental health, estate, miscellaneous civil.
- Misdemeanor, DWI/DUI.
- Moving traffic, miscellaneous traffic.   No jury trials

MUNICIPAL COURTS AND THE CITY COURT OF ATLANTA (~390 courts)

- Limited felony, DWI/DUI.
- Traffic, ordinance violation. No jury trials except in Atlanta City Court

JUVENILE COURT (159 counties: 62 separate courts, judges in 97 other counties also sit on other courts) 11 full-time and 40 part-time judges, 2 of whom also serve as State Court judges. Superior Court judges serve in the 97 remaining counties without a separate Juvenile Court judge.

- Moving traffic, miscellaneous traffic.
- Juvenile.   No jury trials

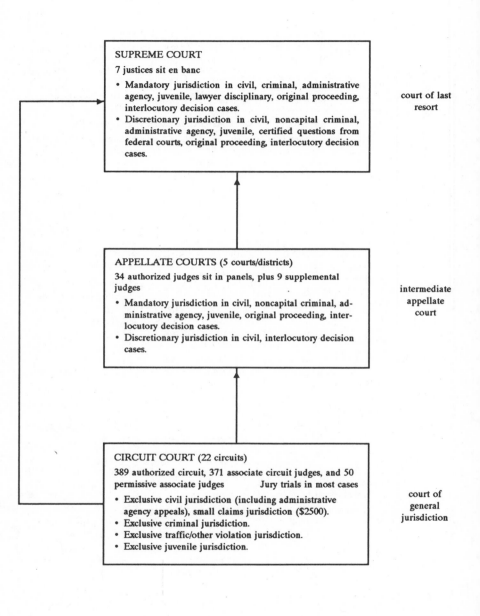

SUPREME COURT

7 justices sit en banc

- Mandatory jurisdiction in civil, criminal, administrative agency, juvenile, lawyer disciplinary, original proceeding, interlocutory decision cases.
- Discretionary jurisdiction in civil, noncapital criminal, administrative agency, juvenile, certified questions from federal courts, original proceeding, interlocutory decision cases.

court of last resort

APPELLATE COURTS (5 courts/districts)

34 authorized judges sit in panels, plus 9 supplemental judges

- Mandatory jurisdiction in civil, noncapital criminal, administrative agency, juvenile, original proceeding, interlocutory decision cases.
- Discretionary jurisdiction in civil, interlocutory decision cases.

intermediate appellate court

CIRCUIT COURT (22 circuits)

389 authorized circuit, 371 associate circuit judges, and 50 permissive associate judges   Jury trials in most cases

- Exclusive civil jurisdiction (including administrative agency appeals), small claims jurisdiction ($2500).
- Exclusive criminal jurisdiction.
- Exclusive traffic/other violation jurisdiction.
- Exclusive juvenile jurisdiction.

court of general jurisdiction

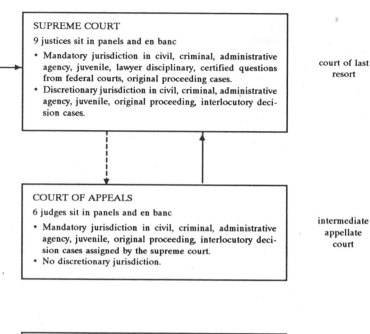

SUPREME COURT

9 justices sit in panels and en banc
- Mandatory jurisdiction in civil, criminal, administrative agency, juvenile, lawyer disciplinary, certified questions from federal courts, original proceeding cases.
- Discretionary jurisdiction in civil, criminal, administrative agency, juvenile, original proceeding, interlocutory decision cases.

court of last resort

COURT OF APPEALS

6 judges sit in panels and en banc
- Mandatory jurisdiction in civil, criminal, administrative agency, juvenile, original proceeding, interlocutory decision cases assigned by the supreme court.
- No discretionary jurisdiction.

intermediate appellate court

DISTRICT COURT (8 districts in 99 counties)

100 judges, 42 district associate judges, 19 senior judges, and 158 part-time magistrates
- Exclusive civil jurisdiction (including trial court appeals). Small claims jurisdiction ($2000).
- Exclusive criminal jurisdiction (including criminal appeals).
- Exclusive traffic/other violation jurisdiction, except for uncontested parking.
- Exclusive juvenile jurisdiction.

Jury trials, except in small claims, juvenile, equity cases, city and county ordinance violations, and mental health cases.

court of general jurisdiction

– – – – – – Indicates assignment of cases.

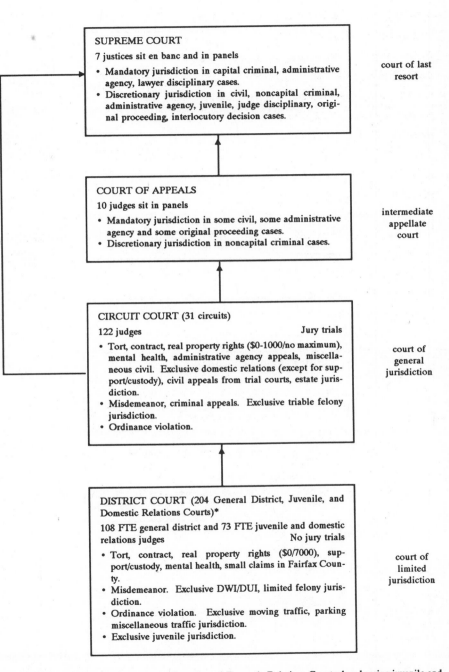

SUPREME COURT

7 justices sit en banc and in panels
- Mandatory jurisdiction in capital criminal, administrative agency, lawyer disciplinary cases.
- Discretionary jurisdiction in civil, noncapital criminal, administrative agency, juvenile, judge disciplinary, original proceeding, interlocutory decision cases.

court of last resort

COURT OF APPEALS

10 judges sit in panels
- Mandatory jurisdiction in some civil, some administrative agency and some original proceeding cases.
- Discretionary jurisdiction in noncapital criminal cases.

intermediate appellate court

CIRCUIT COURT (31 circuits)

122 judges   Jury trials
- Tort, contract, real property rights ($0-1000/no maximum), mental health, administrative agency appeals, miscellaneous civil. Exclusive domestic relations (except for support/custody), civil appeals from trial courts, estate jurisdiction.
- Misdemeanor, criminal appeals. Exclusive triable felony jurisdiction.
- Ordinance violation.

court of general jurisdiction

DISTRICT COURT (204 General District, Juvenile, and Domestic Relations Courts)*

108 FTE general district and 73 FTE juvenile and domestic relations judges   No jury trials
- Tort, contract, real property rights ($0/7000), support/custody, mental health, small claims in Fairfax County.
- Misdemeanor. Exclusive DWI/DUI, limited felony jurisdiction.
- Ordinance violation. Exclusive moving traffic, parking miscellaneous traffic jurisdiction.
- Exclusive juvenile jurisdiction.

court of limited jurisdiction

*The District Court is referred to as the Juvenile and Domestic Relations Court when hearing juvenile and domestic relations cases, and as the General District Court for the balance of cases.

APPENDIX B

THE COURTS OF THE FIFTY STATES

Courts of Last Resort
Intermediate Appellate Courts
Trial Courts of General Jurisdiction

The tables included here are adapted from those contained in *The Book of the States* 1990-91 Edition, pp. 204-7, published by the Council of State Governments, Lexington, Kentucky.

Courts of Last Resort

State	Name	Judges	Term*
Alabama	Supreme Court	9	6
Alaska	Supreme Court	5	10
Arizona	Supreme Court	5	6
Arkansas	Supreme Court	7	8
California	Supreme Court	7	12
Colorado	Supreme Court	7	10
Connecticut	Supreme Court	7	8
Delaware	Supreme Court	5	12
Florida	Supreme Court	7	6
Georgia	Supreme Court	7	6
Hawaii	Supreme Court	5	10
Idaho	Supreme Court	5	6
Illinois	Supreme Court	7	10
Indiana	Supreme Court	5	10
Iowa	Supreme Court	9	8
Kansas	Supreme Court	7	6
Kentucky	Supreme Court	7	8
Louisiana	Supreme Court	7	10
Maine	Supreme Judicial Court	7	7
Maryland	Court of Appeals	7	10
Massachusetts	Supreme Judicial Court	7	To age 70
Michigan	Supreme Court	7	8
Minnesota	Supreme Court	7	6
Mississippi	Supreme Court	9	8
Missouri	Supreme Court	7	12
Montana	Supreme Court	7	8

Courts of Last Resort

State	Name	Judges	Term*
Nebraska	Supreme Court	7	6
Nevada	Supreme Court	5	6
New Hampshire	Supreme Court	5	To age 70
New Jersey	Supreme Court	7	7
New Mexico	Supreme Court	5	8
New York	Court of Appeals	7	14
North Carolina	Supreme Court	7	8
North Dakota	Supreme Court	5	10
Ohio	Supreme Court	7	6
Oklahoma	Supreme Court	9	6
	Court of Criminal Appeals	3	6
Oregon	Supreme Court	7	6
Pennsylvania	Supreme Court	7	10
Rhode Island	Supreme Court	5	Life
South Carolina	Supreme Court	5	10
South Dakota	Supreme Court	5	8
Tennessee	Supreme Court	5	8
Texas	Supreme Court	9	6
	Court of Criminal Appeals	9	6
Utah	Supreme Court	5	10
Vermont	Supreme Court	5	6
Virginia	Supreme Court	7	12
Washington	Supreme Court	9	6
West Virginia	Supreme Court	5	12
Wisconsin	Supreme Court	7	10
Wyoming	Supreme Court	5	8

*The terms shown are in years.

Intermediate Appellate Courts

State	Name	Judges	Term*
Alabama	Court of Criminal Appeals	5	6
	Court of Civil Appeals	3	6
Alaska	Court of Appeals	3	8
Arizona	Courts of Appeals	18	6
Arkansas	Court of Appeals	6	8
California	Courts of Appeal	88	12
Colorado	Court of Appeals	13	8
Connecticut	Appellate Court	9	8
Delaware	...	...	...
Florida	District Courts of Appeals	46	6
Georgia	Court of Appeals	9	6
Hawaii	Intermediate Court of Appeals	3	10
Idaho	Court of Appeals	3	6
Illinois	Appellate Courts	34	10
Indiana	Court of Appeals	12	10
Iowa	Court of Appeals	6	6
Kansas	Court of Appeals	10	4
Kentucky	Court of Appeals	14	8
Louisiana	Courts of Appeals	52	10
Maine	...	...	...
Maryland	Court of Special Appeals	13	10
Massachusetts	Appeals Court	14	To age 70
Michigan	Court of Appeals	18	6
Minnesota	Court of Appeals	13	6
Mississippi	...	...	...
Missouri	Courts of Appeals	32	12
Montana	...	...	...

Intermediate Appellate Courts

State	Name	Judges	Term*
Nebraska	...	...	...
Nevada	...	...	...
New Hampshire	...	...	...
New Jersey	Appellate Division, Superior Court	28	7
New Mexico	Court of Appeals	7	8
New York	Appellate Divisions, Supreme Court	47	5
	Appellate Terms, Supreme Court	15	5
North Carolina	Court of Appeals	12	8
North Dakota	Court of Appeals (temporary)	3	...
Ohio	Courts of Appeals	59	6
Oklahoma	Courts of Appeals	12	6
Oregon	Court of Appeals	10	6
	Tax Court	1	6
Pennsylvania	Superior Court	15	10
	Commonwealth Court	9	10
Rhode Island	...	...	...
South Carolina	Court of Appeals	6	6
South Dakota	...	...	...
Tennessee	Court of Appeals	12	8
	Court of Criminal Appeals	9	8
Texas	Courts of Appeals	80	6
Utah	Court of Appeals	7	10
Vermont	...	...	...
Virginia	Court of Appeals	10	8
Washington	Courts of Appeals	16	6
West Virginia	...	...	...
Wisconsin	Courts of Appeals	13	6
Wyoming	...	...	...

*The terms shown are in years.

Trial Courts of General Jurisdiction
(trial courts of limited jurisdiction not included)

State	Name	Judges	Term*
Alabama	Circuit Court	124	6
Alaska	Superior Court	30	6
Arizona	Superior Court	101	4
Arkansas	Chancery Court	34	4
	Circuit Court	33	6
California	Superior Court	725	6
Colorado	District Court	110	6
Connecticut	Superior Court	139	8
Delaware	Superior Court	15	12
Florida	Circuit Court	372	6
Georgia	Superior Court	137	4
Hawaii	Circuit Court	24	10
Idaho	District Court	33	4
Illinois	Circuit Court	760	6
Indiana	Superior Court	129	6
	Circuit Court	90	6
Iowa	District Court	100	6
Kansas	District Court	146	4
Kentucky	Circuit Court	91	8
Louisiana	District Court	192	6
Maine	Superior Court	16	7
Maryland	Circuit Court	109	15
Massachusetts	Trial Court	320	To age 70
Michigan	Circuit Court	167	6
Minnesota	District Court	230	6
Mississippi	Chancery Court	39	4
	Circuit Court	40	4
Missouri	Circuit Court	133	6
Montana	District Court	36	6

Trial Courts of General Jurisdiction
(trial courts of limited jurisdiction not included)

State	Name	Judges	Term*
Nebraska	District Court	48	6
Nevada	District Court	39	6
New Hampshire	Superior Court	25	To age 70
New Jersey	Superior Court	349	7
New Mexico	District Court	59	6
New York	Supreme Court	484	14
North Carolina	Superior Court	74	8
North Dakota	District Court	27	6
Ohio	Court of Common Pleas	344	6
Oklahoma	District Court	71	4
Oregon	Circuit Court	87	6
Pennsylvania	Court of Common Pleas	341	10
Rhode Island	Superior Court	20	Life
South Carolina	Circuit Court	31	6
South Dakota	Circuit Court	35	8
Tennessee	Chancery Court	35	8
	Circuit Court	97	8
Texas	District Court	385	4
Utah	District Court	29	6
Vermont	Superior Court	10	6
	District Court	15	6
Virginia	Circuit Court	122	8
Washington	Superior Court	136	4
West Virginia	Circuit Court	60	8
Wisconsin	Circuit Court	208	6
Wyoming	District Court	17	6

*The terms shown are in years.

THE FEDERAL COURTS

This table includes the Supreme Court, courts of appeals, and district courts. It does not include other federal courts. The city shown by each court of appeals is the location of the court's headquarters; however, in many circuits the court also sits from time to time in other cities in the circuit.

The information in this table is found in 28 U.S.C. §§ 44, 133. The table includes all authorized judgeships for the district courts and courts of appeals as of January 1991.

	Judges
Supreme Court (Washington, D.C.)	9
1st Circuit	
Court of Appeals (Boston, MA)	6
District Courts	
District of Maine	3
District of Massachusetts	13
District of New Hampshire	3
District of Puerto Rico	7
District of Rhode Island	3
2nd Circuit	
Court of Appeals (New York, NY)	13
District Courts	
District of Connecticut	8
Northern District of New York	4
Southern District of New York	28
Eastern District of New York	15
Western District of New York	4
District of Vermont	2
3rd Circuit	
Court of Appeals (Philadelphia, PA)	14
District Courts	
District of Delaware	4
District of New Jersey	17
Eastern District of Pennsylvania	22
Middle District of Pennsylvania	6
Western District of Pennsylvania	10
4th Circuit	
Court of Appeals (Richmond, VA)	15
District Courts	
District of Maryland	10
Eastern District of North Carolina	4
Middle District of North Carolina	4
Western District of North Carolina	3
District of South Carolina	9
Eastern District of Virginia	9
Western District of Virginia	4
Northern District of West Virginia	3
Southern District of West Virginia	5

	Judges
5th Circuit	
Court of Appeals (New Orleans, LA)	17
District Courts	
Eastern District of Louisiana	13
Middle District of Louisiana	2
Western District of Louisiana	7
Northern District of Mississippi	3
Southern District of Mississippi	6
Northern District of Texas	12
Eastern District of Texas	7
Southern District of Texas	18
Western District of Texas	10
6th Circuit	
Court of Appeals (Cincinnati, OH)	16
District Courts	
Eastern District of Kentucky	4
Western District of Kentucky	4
Eastern & Western Districts of Kentucky*	1
Eastern District of Michigan	15
Western District of Michigan	4
Northern District of Ohio	11
Southern District of Ohio	8
Eastern District of Tennessee	5
Middle District of Tennessee	4
Western District of Tennessee	5
7th Circuit	
Court of Appeals (Chicago, IL)	11
District Courts	
Northern District of Illinois	22
Central District of Illinois	3
Southern District of Illinois	3
Northern District of Indiana	5
Southern District of Indiana	5
Eastern District of Wisconsin	4
Western District of Wisconsin	2
8th Circuit	
Court of Appeals (St. Louis, MO)	11
District Courts	
Eastern District of Arkansas	5

	Judges
Western District of Arkansas	3
Northern District of Iowa	2
Southern District of Iowa	3
District of Minnesota	7
Eastern District of Missouri	6
Western District of Missouri	5
Eastern & Western Districts of Missouri*	2
District of Nebraska	3
District of North Dakota	2
District of South Dakota	3

9th Circuit
Court of Appeals (San Francisco, CA)	28
District Courts	
District of Alaska	3
District of Arizona	8
Northern District of California	14
Eastern District of California	6
Central District of California	27
Southern District of California	8
District of Hawaii	3
District of Idaho	2
District of Montana	3
District of Nevada	4
District of Oregon	6
Eastern District of Washington	4
Western District of Washington	7

10th Circuit
Court of Appeals (Denver, CO)	12
District Courts	
District of Colorado	7
District of Kansas	5
District of New Mexico	5
Northern District of Oklahoma	3
Eastern District of Oklahoma	1
Western District of Oklahoma	6
Eastern, Western & Northern Districts of Oklahoma*	1
District of Utah	5
District of Wyoming	3

	Judges
11th Circuit	
Court of Appeals (Atlanta, GA)	12
District Courts	
Northern District of Alabama	7
Middle District of Alabama	3
Southern District of Alabama	3
Northern District of Florida	4
Middle District of Florida	11
Southern District of Florida	16
Northern District of Georgia	11
Middle District of Georgia	4
Southern District of Georgia	3
District of Columbia Circuit	
Court of Appeals (Washington, D.C.)	12
District Court	
District of the District of Columbia	15
Federal Circuit	
Court of Appeals (Washington, D.C.)	12

*This is not a judicial district; it is a designation for a "roving judgeship," an additional judge to serve more than one district.

Note: The numbers shown here represent the active judgeships authorized for each court. However, federal judges, after specified lengths of service and at designated ages, can acquire "senior status." In such status they can continue to sit on their courts if requested to do so. Thus, the actual number of judges participating in each court's work is often greater than the number shown here.

ARTICLE III OF THE UNITED STATES CONSTITUTION

Section 1. The judicial Power of the United States, shall be vested in one supreme Court, and in such inferior Courts as the Congress may from time to time ordain and establish. The Judges, both of the supreme and inferior Courts, shall hold their Offices during good Behaviour, and shall, at stated Times, receive for their Services, a Compensation, which shall not be diminished during their Continuance in Office.

Section 2. The judicial Power shall extend to all Cases, in Law and Equity, arising under this Constitution, the Laws of the United States, and Treaties made, or which shall be made, under their Authority;—to all Cases affecting Ambassadors, other public Ministers and Consuls;—to all Cases of admiralty and maritime Jurisdiction;—to Controversies to which the United States shall be a Party;—to Controversies between two or more States;—between a State and Citizens of another State;—between Citizens of different States;—between Citizens of the same State claiming Lands under Grants of different States, and between a State, or the Citizens thereof, and foreign States, Citizens or Subjects.

In all Cases affecting Ambassadors, other public Ministers and Consuls, and those in which a State shall be Party, the supreme Court shall have original Jurisdiction. In all the other Cases before mentioned, the supreme Court shall have appellate Jurisdiction, both as to Law and Fact, with such Exceptions, and under such Regulations as the Congress shall make.

The Trial of all Crimes, except in Cases of Impeachment, shall be by Jury; and such Trial shall be held in the State where the said Crimes shall have been committed; but when not committed within any State, the Trial shall be at such Place or Places as the Congress may by Law have directed.

Section 3. Treason against the United States, shall consist only in levying War against them, or in adhering to their Enemies, giving them Aid and Comfort. No Person shall be convicted of Treason unless on the Testimony of two Witnesses to the same overt Act, or on Confession in open Court.

The Congress shall have Power to declare the Punishment of Treason, but no Attainder of Treason shall work Corruption of Blood, or Forfeiture except during the Life of the Person attainted.

APPENDIX E

SUGGESTED READINGS AND SOURCES

For a short but comprehensive description of American law and courts, see E. Allan Farnsworth, *An Introduction to the Legal System of the United States*, 2d ed. (Oceana Publications, Inc., 1983). A report entitled *The Role of Courts in American Society* (West Publishing Co., 1984), produced by the Council on the Role of Courts, presents a contemporary picture of the work of state and federal courts and how that work has changed in the course of the twentieth century.

Karl N. Llewellyn's *The Case Law System in America* (University of Chicago Press, 1989), adapted from a series of lectures delivered to a German audience, gives a useful insight into the common-law system. Henry J. Abraham's *The Judicial Process*, 5th ed. (Oxford University Press, 1986) provides a description of American courts and judges, with comparisons to other countries.

The following one-volume works, designed primarily for use by law students, provide good descriptions of the procedures in civil litigation and of certain associated concepts and doctrines in American courts:

> Fleming James, Jr. and Geoffrey C. Hazard, Jr., *Civil Procedure*, 3d ed. (Little, Brown & Co., 1985);
> Jack H. Friedenthal, Mary Kay Kane, & Arthur R. Miller, *Civil Procedure* (West Publishing Co., 1985);
> Delmar Karlen, *Civil Litigation* (Bobbs-Merrill Co., 1978).

Similar works on criminal procedure include the following:

> Wayne R. LaFave & Jerold H. Israel, *Criminal Procedure* (West Publishing Co., 1985);
> Kenneth M. Wells & Paul B. Weston, *Criminal Procedure and Trial Practice* (Prentice-Hall, Inc., 1977).

The appellate process and the workings of appellate courts are addressed in the following:

> Paul D. Carrington, Daniel J. Meador, & Maurice Rosenberg, *Justice on Appeal* (West Publishing Co., 1976);
>
> Robert L. Stern, *Appellate Practice in the United States*, 2d ed. (Bureau of National Affairs, Inc., 1989);
>
> Thomas B. Marvell, *Appellate Courts and Lawyers* (Greenwood Press, 1978).

The jurisdiction of the federal courts and certain procedures in those courts, including problems concerning the relations between federal and state courts, are dealt with in the following:

> Charles Alan Wright, *The Law of Federal Courts*, 4th ed. (West Publishing Co., 1983);
>
> Erwin Chemerinsky, *Federal Jurisdiction* (Little, Brown & Co., 1989).

The contemporary problems in the work of the federal courts are canvassed in Richard A. Posner, *The Federal Courts* (Harvard University Press, 1985).

Statistical data on cases in all federal courts are collected and published annually in the *Report of the Director of the Administrative Office of the United States Courts*. The address of that office is 811 Vermont Avenue, N.W., Washington, D.C. 20544.

The Federal Judicial Center publishes studies and reports concerning the federal courts. Its address is 1520 H Street, N.W., Washington, D.C. 20005.

Statistics on state court business and information about state judicial structures are collected and published periodically by the

National Center for State Courts. The most recent publication is *State Court Caseload Statistics: Annual Report 1988.* The address of the National Center is 300 Newport Avenue, Williamsburg, Virginia 23187.

The American Judicature Society has published a variety of reports concerning judicial selection and conduct, court structures, and judicial administration. Its address is 25 East Washington, Suite 1600, Chicago, Illinois 60602.

Information about courts and judges is maintained by the Judicial Administration Division, American Bar Association, 750 North Lake Shore Drive, 10th Floor, Chicago, Illinois 60611.

National programs of judicial education are provided by and information on judicial education is available from the National Judicial College, Judicial College Building, University of Nevada, Reno, Nevada 89557, and the American Academy of Judicial Education, 1613 15th Street, Tuscaloosa, Alabama 35404. Educational programs and information concerning court administration are available at the Institute for Court Management, 1331 17th Street, Suite 402, Denver, Colorado 80202. Educational programs for appellate judges, as well as research on court problems, are conducted by the Institute of Judicial Administration, 1 Washington Square Village, Suite 1A, New York, NY 10012.

Reports and studies on various aspects of state courts are available from the State Justice Institute, 1650 King Street, Alexandria, Virginia 22314.

INDEX

About the Author . . .

Daniel John Meador is and has been for many years the James Monroe Professor of Law at the University of Virginia. His teaching and research interests have centered on the courts and their processes in the United States, as well as in England and Germany. He has been involved in numerous projects to improve the administration of justice.

He served as Director of the Appellate Justice Project of the National Center for State Courts (1972-74) and as Vice Chairman of the American Bar Association's Action Commission to Reduce Court Costs and Delay (1979-84). He was a member of the Advisory Council on Apppellate Justice (1971-75) and of the Council on the Role of Courts (1979-83). From 1977 to 1979 he was Assistant Attorney General in charge of the Office for Improvements in the Administration of Justice in the United States Department of Justice. In addition to his teaching responsibilities, he has served as Director of the Graduate Program for Judges at the University of Virginia School of Law since 1979. He is currently a member of the Board of Directors of the State Justice Institute.

Professor Meador's books include *Preludes to Gideon: Notes on Appellate Advocacy, Habeas Corpus, and Constitutional Litigation* (1967), *Criminal Appeals: English Practices and American Reforms* (1973), *Appellate Justice: Staff and Process in the Crisis of Volume* (1974), *Mr. Justice Black and His Books* (1974), *Justice on Appeal* (1976, with P. Carrington and M. Rosenberg), and *Impressions of Law in East Germany* (1986).